W9-BVV-499

Scored for Listening: A Guide to Music

GUY ALAN BOCKMON

WILLIAM J. STARR

University of Tennessee

Scored

for Listening:

A Guide

to Music

BRIAR CLIFF COLLEGE
LIBRARY

SIOUX CITY, IOWA

Harcourt, Brace and Company HB *New York*

MT
6
.B649
S4

© 1959, by Harcourt, Brace and Company, Inc.

All rights reserved. No part of this book may be reproduced
in any form, by mimeograph or any other means,
without permission in writing from the publisher.

Library of Congress Catalog Card Number: 59-9799

[a · 4 · 59]

Printed in the United States of America

Preface

This book is in several ways an unusual introductory guide to music. Our aim in preparing it has been twofold: first, to provide a text which focuses upon music rather than upon information about music and, secondly, to offer to the instructor a concise, factual basis upon which he can build his own course. Although this text furnishes materials helpful to the concert-goer or hi-fi enthusiast who wishes to acquire a better understanding of music on his own, it does not usurp the teacher's traditional role of commenting, evaluating, and explaining.

The most distinctive feature of the book is the abundance of annotated Line Scores, which on a single staff (and occasionally on two or more staves) trace throughout musical works the continuous course of principal melodic ideas. Our students at the University of Tennessee readily learn to follow (not to read) these one-line scores, and they derive considerable satisfaction from doing so. Following the scores substitutes active participation for passive—and sometimes inattentive—listening, aids memory and understanding by association of sound with sight, and offers an exact answer to the students anguished cry, "But what do we listen *for?*" The Line Scores are a convenience for the instructor as well, relieving him of the search for scores or the need to analyze from sound.

In addition to the Line Scores, we have included a number of Abbreviated Analyses, in which the illustrated thematic material, linked by explanatory text, forms an outline of the work that can easily be followed step by step. In some cases these verbal links are the composer's original program notes.

32321

The criteria for selection of each work appearing as Line Scores and Abbreviated Analyses have been: Is it a clear example of what it represents as a form or type of composition? Is it in the standard repertory? Is it available on long-playing records? Can it be reduced to one or two lines of melody? Aware that there is today a tremendous increase of interest in music before and after the Romantic period, we have offered extensive coverage of this older and newer music. The major emphasis, however, has been placed on nineteenth-century works which constitute the largest part of the current repertory. We have included samples of orchestral, choral, chamber, song, and keyboard literature.

The text portion of the book, in the form of brief outlines, presents first the materials of music and the ways in which composers use these materials to construct the standard forms and types of musical compositions. Musical examples and listening suggestions are included wherever they can be useful. In the interests of brevity and clarity, we have indulged in some intentional and, we hope, judicious oversimplifications. For example, the difference between a ternary form and a first rondo is very confusing to most non-musicians, so we make no mention of first rondo form.

The final six outlines, designed neither as a condensed survey of music literature nor as an abridged history of music, treat the styles of the six major periods in the development of music. Biographies of composers and discussions of historical backgrounds have been omitted, since this information is readily available as outside reading. We have concentrated instead upon the music. Each of these last six outlines begins with a general discussion of the characteristic sound of the music, followed by a more detailed treatment of the typical performance media, rhythm, melody, texture, and structure of the music of the period. Each major composer's style is then commented upon. Finally, for the student who wishes to explore further on his own, a list of other composers is provided, with one or two representative works suggested for each. The division of composers into just six outlines is, as instructors will recognize, another example of judicious oversimplification.

Throughout, we have tried to design the book to be easily adaptable to the teacher's individual instruction techniques and to the needs of the students in his classroom. For example, because the outlines are relatively independent of each other, it is possible to vary the order in which they are taken up. Some instructors, for instance, may prefer to begin the study of the musical styles section with the Romantic period, in accordance with the "familiar to unknown" principle. It will be found, too, that the outlines can be reduced easily to meet the needs of a short course. Also, we have wherever possible avoided suggesting value judgments and taking sides in scholarly disputes, which we feel strongly to be the province of the individual teacher—and of the student himself.

We wish to thank Professors Alfred L. Schmied and David Van Vactor of the University of Tennessee, Professor Jan LaRue of New York University, and Professor Howard A. Murphy of Teachers College, Columbia University, for their suggestions on various portions of the book; Professor Hugo Magliocco of Knoxville College and Dr. Rolf-Dieter Pohl for their translations of Italian and German texts; and the members of the staff of the James D. Hoskins Library for their courteous assistance. We are especially grateful to Professor George F. Devine of the University of Tennessee for his criticism of the entire manuscript and to Constance Starr and Sue Callis Bockmon for their patience and assistance during its preparation.

G.A.B.

W.J.S.

Knoxville, Tennessee

March, 1959

How to Follow
the Line Scores

The Line Scores in this book are intended to increase the listener's enjoyment and understanding of music by heightening his perception of the composer's musical ideas. A facility in connecting musical sound with notation is not difficult to acquire. To make profitable use of the Line Scores, it is not necessary to be able to read music as a musician does when playing or singing, but only to be able to follow the music as it is being played.

Musical notation employs symbols placed on a five-line staff. These symbols indicate both the pitch and duration of musical sounds. While most of the scores in this book have been reduced to one staff, it is sometimes necessary to use two or more staves joined at both ends by vertical lines. It is important to remember in following the scores that the music in staves so joined is being performed simultaneously.

The first step in learning to follow musical notation is to recognize the relationship between the rise and fall of the tones heard and the rise and fall of the notes on the staff. The words "high" and "low" are commonly used to refer to the pitch of tones, and musical notation follows this terminology. Higher tones are indicated by notes placed higher on the staff. The general range of pitch is indicated by the clef sign at the beginning of the staff. The treble clef 𝄞 shows that the music is in the higher range, while the bass clef 𝄢 indicates the lower range of pitch.

The listener following the Line Scores needs to be aware only of the direction of the line of music rather than the exact pitches. For example, the direction of the melodic line can be observed as these melodies are sung:

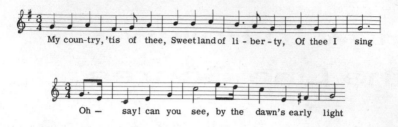

The next step in learning to follow music is to observe the rhythmic flow of the musical sounds. In most instances, beats are grouped in twos or threes, each group of beats consisting of an accented (strong) beat followed by one or more unaccented (weak) beats. These regularly recurring groups of strong and weak beats produce what is called *meter*.

If the beats are tapped out for the above example from "America," they are felt in groups of threes. This is called *triple meter:* one strong beat followed by two weaker beats.

The following example is in *duple meter*. The beats are grouped in twos: a strong beat followed by a weaker one.

Vertical lines on the staff, called bar lines, mark off groups of beats into *measures* or *bars*. Each regular measure, regardless of the number of notes it contains, consists of the same number of beats. The number of beats in a measure is indicated by the top number of the *meter signature*—$\frac{3}{4}$ or $\frac{2}{4}$, for example—which is found at the beginning of the score.

If the beats move very rapidly, the ear may tend to group them into a larger unit; if they move very slowly the beats may be divided and their subdivisions felt as beats. The following example is in duple meter. If it is sung or

Animato.   Animated.
Appassionata.   Passionately.
A tempo.   Returning to original tempo.
D.C.   *Da capo* (see Index).
Dolce.   Sweet, soft.
Espressivo.   Expressive.
f *(Forte).*   Loud.
ff *(Fortissimo).*   Very loud.
Feroce.   Fierce.
Fuoco.   Fiery, passionate.
Furioso.   Furious.
Giusto.   Exact, precise.
Grazioso.   Gracefully.
Larghetto.   Not as slowly as largo.
Lento.   Slowly.
Maestoso.   Majestically.
Marcia.   A march.
Marziale.   March-like.
Meno.   Less.
mf *(Mezzo forte).*   Medium loud.
mp *(Mezzo piano).*   Medium soft.
Molto.   Much, very.
Mosso, (con) moto.   (With) motion.
p *(Piano).*   Soft.
pp *(Pianissimo).*   Very soft.
Piu.   More.
Poco.   Little.
Recit.   Recitative (see Index).
Rit. (Ritardando).   Retard.
Sempre.   Always.
Sentimento.   Sentiment.
Sostenuto.   Sustained.
Tempo I.   In the first tempo.
Tranquillo.   Tranquil.
Vivo.   Animated.

The treble, or G, clef. The second line of the staff is designated as G above middle C. (Music for tenors utilizes this clef, but the pitches heard are one octave lower than those written.)

The bass, or F, clef. The fourth line of the staff is designated as F below middle C.

The C clef. This clef may appear on different lines of the staff. Wherever placed, it marks the position of middle C—in this instance on the third line.

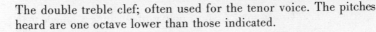 The double treble clef; often used for the tenor voice. The pitches heard are one octave lower than those indicated.

 Sharp (see Index).

 Flat (see Index).

 Natural. Nullifies a sharp or flat.

 Double sharp. Raises the pitch of a note two half-steps.

 Fermata. Hold, or pause. Indicates a considerable lengthening of a note.

 Accent marks.

 Sforzando indications. Performed with marked and sudden emphasis.

 Forte piano. Strong accent, diminishing instantly to piano.

 Dot. Indicates staccato (see Index).

 Trill (see Index).

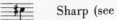 Turn. A melodic ornamentation.

 Triplet. A group of three equal notes to be performed in the time of two.

Grace note. A short note embellishing a longer note.

   Tremolo (see Index).

   Repeat signs. The measures between the two signs are
to be repeated.

First and second endings; the two endings for a
repeated passage.

Contents

Introduction

The substance of music is sound, the sensation produced in the ear when vibrations are set up in the surrounding air. The composer puts together sounds which he hears imaginatively. He may perform his work immediately (improvisation) or he may commit it to a *score*, a written record of his creation.

Just as a blueprint is not a building, so a score is not music. The builder's special skills are needed for the blueprint specifications to be realized in wood, metal, or masonry. The performer's special skills are needed for the score specifications to be realized in actual sound. No amount of reading about, talking about, or looking at music can replace for the listener his active participation as an auditor of musical performances.

A musical composition consists of complex combinations of sounds. A single isolated sound may possess four characteristics: *volume*, perceived as "loud" or "soft"; *quality*, which enables the listener to distinguish between sounds produced by different sources; *duration*, or length in time, of vibration; and *pitch*, perceived as "high" or "low."

Volume is used musically in relatively simple ways. The degree of loudness is usually indicated by Italian words. *Forte* (loud) and *piano* (soft) are used alone or combined with such qualifying terms as *mezzo* (medium) or the suffix *-issimo* (which yields the superlative "-est"). Changes from loud to soft may be accomplished by sudden contrast or gradually through *crescendo* (increasing volume) or *diminuendo* (decreasing volume).

Quality, duration, and pitch are utilized in music according to fairly complicated principles which are discussed at some length in Parts 1, 2, and 3 of this book.

1

part 1

Timbre

If two tones of identical volume, pitch, and duration are produced, one by whistling and the other by singing, the difference in quality is sufficient to enable the listener to distinguish between the two sounds. The quality of sound, dependent upon the complexity of the sound wave, is the physical basis of *timbre* or *tone color* in music.

The timbre of one human voice or of one musical instrument is relatively limited, although there is some difference in timbre between extremely high and low tones, very loud and very soft tones, and "straight" tones and those warmed by *vibrato* (intentional, slight, rapid fluctuations of pitch). Combinations of timbre on the other hand, constitute an almost inexhaustible source of color contrasts.

1

The Human Voice

Singing, which originated as an intensification of speech, is perhaps the oldest medium of musical expression. Voices may be classified by the singer's sex, range, and by the type of literature performed.

I. Soprano. The soprano is the highest-pitched voice. Soloists are classified by the kind of literature they perform.

    A. COLORATURA. A coloratura specializes in rapid passages, runs, trills (rapid alternation of adjacent pitches), and similar vocal acrobatics.

    SUGGESTED LISTENING—Mozart: Queen of the Night's aria ("Vengeance Aria") from *The Magic Flute*; Delibes: "Bell Song" from *Lakme*.

    B. LYRIC. A lyric soprano specializes in slower moving, more tuneful material requiring less agility than the coloratura.

    SUGGESTED LISTENING—Bizet: Micaela's air from *Carmen*; Puccini: "Mi chiamano Mimi" from *La Bohème*.

    C. DRAMATIC. The dramatic soprano specializes in songs of a forceful and declamatory style which require great vocal beauty and power. The dramatic voice lacks the agility of the coloratura and the fragility of the lyric.

    SUGGESTED LISTENING—Wagner: "Liebestod" from *Tristan und Isolde*; Beethoven: "Ah Perfido."

II. Mezzo-soprano. The mezzo-soprano is the medium-pitched female voice.

    SUGGESTED LISTENING—Bizet: "Habanera" from *Carmen*; Saint-Saëns: "My Heart at Thy Sweet Voice" from *Samson and Delilah*.

III. Alto or contralto. The alto is the lowest-pitched female voice.

    SUGGESTED LISTENING—Handel: "He Shall Feed His Flock" from *Messiah*; Brahms: *Alto Rhapsody*.

IV. Tenor. The tenor is the highest-pitched natural male voice. Soloists are classified by the literature they perform.

A. LYRIC. The lyric tenor specializes in tuneful and rather slow-moving melodies.

SUGGESTED LISTENING—Puccini: "Che gelida manina" from *La Bohème;* Verdi: "La donna e mobile" from *Rigoletto.*

B. DRAMATIC. The dramatic tenor specializes in literature of a forceful and declamatory nature.

SUGGESTED LISTENING—Leoncavallo: "Vesti la giubba" from *I Pagliacci;* Verdi: "Celeste Aida" from *Aida.*

V. Baritone. The baritone is the medium-pitched male voice.

SUGGESTED LISTENING—Bizet: "Toreador song" from *Carmen;* Verdi: "Di Provenza il mar" from *La Traviata.*

VI. Bass. The bass is the lowest-pitched male voice. Bass soloists are further classified by range.

A. BASS-BARITONE. The bass-baritone lacks the low pitches of the bass and the high pitches of the baritone.

SUGGESTED LISTENING—Moussorgsky: "Hallucination scene" and "Death scene" from *Boris Godounov.*

B. BASSO. The basso capitalizes upon his extremely low pitches.

SUGGESTED LISTENING—Mozart: "In These Sacred Halls" from *The Magic Flute;* Gounod: "Calf of Gold" song from *Faust.*

VII. Other voices include *boy soprano,* the high-pitched voice of the pre-adolescent male; *cambiata,* the "changing" voice of the adolescent male; *castrato,* the adult male whose change of voice is prevented surgically (not practiced in this century); and *countertenor,* the adult male who cultivates the use of *falsetto* (false voice) to sing in a range higher than that of the tenor.

2

Musical Instruments

Although any object which can be made to produce sound could conceivably be called a musical instrument, only a limited number of such objects are in common use. They are usually categorized as *string, wind, percussion* or *keyboard* instruments.

I. **Strings.** The tones of stringed instruments are produced by plucking or bowing taut strings.

    A. INSTRUMENTS PLAYED WITH A BOW. Most of the stringed instruments used in concert music are usually played with a bow, but they may also be plucked. *Arco* and *pizzicato* indicate bowed and plucked passages, respectively. *Double, triple,* or *quadruple stops* are produced by playing simultaneously on two or more strings. Greater expression and color may be produced by using *vibrato.* An agitated effect results from *tremolo* (rapid iteration of a pitch). A *mute (sordino)* is a device used to decrease the resonance of the sound.

        1. VIOLIN. The smallest (23 inches long) and highest-pitched bowed instrument normally plays the soprano or alto part. The timbre is the standard with which that of the other bowed stringed instruments is compared. The violin is one of the most intimate, flexible, and expressive instruments, capable of performing rapid passages, heavily accented rhythmic effects, lovely sustained melodies, capricious skips and leaps, dramatic tremolos, and dynamic gradations from a whisper to a full strong tone.

        SUGGESTED LISTENING—Rimsky-Korsakov: violin cadenzas in *Scheherazade;* Brahms: 3rd mvt. of *Symphony No. 3;* Weber: Overture to *Oberon.*

        2. VIOLA. The next largest member of this group (26½ inches long) normally plays the tenor part. The timbre is noticeably darker and less incisive than that of the violin and is often used to suggest a mood of nostalgia or sadness.

        SUGGESTED LISTENING—Berlioz: solo viola in *Harold in Italy,* viola with English horn in *Roman Carnival Overture;* Ravel: viola with clarinet at beginning of *Daphnis and Chloe, Suite No. 2;* Tchaikovsky: viola with English horn in *Romeo and Juliet.*

3. CELLO (contraction of *violoncello*). The cello, which normally plays the bass part, is the next largest (49 inches long) instrument. Capable of a wealth of color, the cello timbre is strong and sonorous, midway in brightness between the violin and viola.

SUGGESTED LISTENING—Beethoven: unison with violas in 2nd mvt. of *Symphony No. 5;* Brahms: 3rd mvt. of *Symphony No. 3;* Harris: beginning of *Symphony No. 3.*

4. DOUBLE BASS. As its name implies, the largest instrument (more than 6 feet long) of the group is often used to add strength and depth to the bass part. Its extremely low pitch, lack of agility, and limited expressiveness render the double bass unsuitable for solos of any great length.

SUGGESTED LISTENING—Beethoven: trio from 3rd mvt. of *Symphony No. 5* (with cellos), 4th mvt. of *Symphony No. 9* (with cellos); Saint-Saëns: "The Elephant" from *The Carnival of the Animals.*

B. INSTRUMENTS PLAYED BY PLUCKING THE STRINGS

1. HARP. The harp owes its distinctive timbre in part to its rippling *glissandos* and *arpeggios* in which the tones are heard neither individually nor simultaneously but in a cascade of pitches.

SUGGESTED LISTENING—Tchaikovsky: "Waltz of the Flowers" from *The Nutcracker Suite;* Rimsky-Korsakov: *Capriccio Espagnole;* Debussy: *Prelude to the Afternoon of a Faun.*

2. OTHER PLUCKED INSTRUMENTS. The *guitar, banjo, ukelele,* and *mandolin* are associated with popular entertainment.

II. **Wind instruments.** The wind instruments have been associated traditionally with outdoor functions, particularly martial and sporting. The tones are produced by setting into vibration a column of air within the instrument.

A. WOODWINDS. Some of the woodwinds are now made of metal. The name has survived from an earlier day when they were all made of wood.

1. "EDGE-TONE" (REEDLESS) INSTRUMENTS. The "edge-tone" is produced by blowing across an opening, like "tooting" a bottle. Incapable of the extreme soft tone of the strings but (particularly in the upper register) possessing a penetrating loud tone, the "edge-tone" instruments specialize in fast passages, trills, and rapid runs. They are also valuable for lovely, sustained, middle-register playing. The use of the instruments is limited by the player's breath requirements.

a. FLUTE. The soprano of the family, the flute is used extensively as a melodic instrument and for adding brilliance to the *tutti* (a term meaning "all play"). The timbre is clear and bright, except in the extremely low register where it becomes thick, veiled, and breathy.

SUGGESTED LISTENING—Debussy: *Prelude to the Afternoon of a Faun;* Tchaikovsky: "Dance of the Toy Flutes" from *The Nutcracker Suite;* Brahms: 4th mvt. of *Symphony No. 4.*

b. PICCOLO. The piccolo, half the size of the flute, is the highest-pitched woodwind. The timbre is bright and metallic, the high register adding a brilliant sparkle to the tutti.

SUGGESTED LISTENING—Tchaikovsky: "Chinese Dance" from *The Nutcracker Suite;* Sousa: *Stars and Stripes Forever;* Milhaud: *Suite Provençale.*

c. ALTO FLUTE (sometimes incorrectly called *bass flute*). The alto flute is larger than the standard flute. It retains the clear timbre of the "edge-tone" family, but sounds rich, velvety, dark, and subdued.

2. DOUBLE REEDS. The tones are produced by a pair of reeds, pressed together between the player's lips, set into vibration by an air stream. They are the least agile of the woodwinds. The use of the double reeds is limited by the player's breath capacity and by the endurance of his *embouchure* (playing position of the facial muscles, especially the lips). Double reeds are sometimes used to suggest the Orient.

a. OBOE. The oboe is the soprano of the family. The timbre is so distinctive and penetrating that it is used principally for solos. The timbre is quite delicate and refined, although pungent, nasal, and unmistakable.

SUGGESTED LISTENING—Brahms: 2nd mvt. of *Violin Concerto in D;* Tchaikovsky: 2nd mvt. of *Symphony No. 4;* Berlioz: 3rd mvt. of *Symphonie Fantastique.*

b. ENGLISH HORN. The alto of the family resembles the oboe. Its primary use is in solos, particularly those depicting moods of melancholy and sadness. The timbre of the English horn is a bit coarser, darker, and more penetrating than that of the oboe.

SUGGESTED LISTENING—Franck: 2nd mvt. of *Symphony in D Minor;* Dvořák: 2nd mvt. of *Symphony No. 5;* Berlioz: *Roman Carnival Overture.*

c. BASSOON. The bassoon usually performs the bass part but it may also be used as the tenor. The timbre is pungent, reedy, and sonorous in the middle register. The upper register sounds rather pinched, and the extremely low register has a tendency toward coarseness. The bassoon lends dignity to slow passages, but rapid repeated notes or fast staccato passages usually sound somewhat comical.

SUGGESTED LISTENING—Dukas: *The Sorcerer's Apprentice;* Rimsky-Korsakov: 2nd mvt. of *Scheherazade;* Grieg: "In the Hall of the Mountain King" from *Peer Gynt Suite No. 1.*

d. DOUBLE BASSOON. The double bassoon (also called *contra-bassoon*) lends depth to the bass part.

SUGGESTED LISTENING—Dukas: *The Sorcerer's Apprentice;* Ravel: "Beauty and the Beast" from *Mother Goose Suite;* Strauss: *Death and Transfiguration* (with string basses).

played very rapidly, the two beats of the measure can be easily felt as one beat per measure.

Yan - kee Doo - dle   went   to   town   a - rid - ing   on   a   po - ny

As a result of this rapid movement of beats, meters with 6, 9, and 12 as top numbers in the signature are rarely heard as 6, 9, and 12 beats to the bar, but rather as 2, 3, and 4 beats, because the beats within the measure are grouped in threes. In the following example, two beats per measure are heard rather than the six beats indicated in the signature.

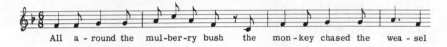

All   a - round the   mul-ber-ry bush   the   mon - key chased the   wea - sel

The next example illustrates how subdivisions may be made when the beats move very slowly. The meter is duple, $\frac{2}{4}$, but the beats move so slowly that it is natural to feel four beats to the bar.

Swing low, sweet   cha - ri - ot___

The speed of the flow of beats is indicated by the *tempo*, which is given at the beginning of a work. A list of basic tempo indications is included in Outline 4.

The listener who has had little or no previous contact with musical notation will find it easiest to follow measure by measure, rather than note by note, remembering that since each measure contains the same number of beats each spans the same amount of time. As measures are followed in this way, many notation symbols will become familiar. The following list explains the terms and symbols used in the Line Scores and Abbreviated Analyses which are not defined elsewhere in the text.

Affettuoso.   Affectionately.
Agitato.   Agitated.
Allegretto.   Moderately fast.
Andantino.   Slightly faster than andante.

3. SINGLE REEDS. The tones are produced by the vibration of one wooden reed.

    a. CLARINET IN B-FLAT OR A. The most important single reed instrument, the clarinet in B-flat or A, is the instrument musicians call, simply, "clarinet." The dynamic possibilities range from the intimate pianissimo to an assertive fortissimo. Rapid passages, trills, and arpeggios are almost as natural for the clarinet as for the flute. The timbre varies from the brilliant clarion upper register to the rich and lush lower register.

    SUGGESTED LISTENING—Brahms: 2nd mvt. of *Symphony No. 3*; Rachmaninoff: 3rd mvt. of *Symphony No. 2*; Respighi: "Pines of the Janiculum" from *Pines of Rome*.

    b. BASS CLARINET. The timbre of the bass clarinet differs from that of its smaller relative in a certain hollowness of sound.

    SUGGESTED LISTENING—Wagner: "King Mark's song" from *Tristan and Isolde*; Stravinsky: "Scene in the Moor's room," from *Petrouchka*; Respighi: "Pines of the Appian Way" from *Pines of Rome*.

    c. OTHER CLARINETS. Other members of the clarinet family include the small *clarinet in E-flat, alto clarinet*, and *contra-bass clarinet*.

    d. SAXOPHONE. Called for only infrequently in serious concert music, the saxophone family includes *sopranino, soprano, alto, tenor, baritone* and *bass*.

B. BRASSES. The tones of the powerful brasses are produced by the player's lips being forced into vibration within a mouthpiece. Less agile than either the strings or the woodwinds, and with smaller pitch range, the brasses have been used in concert music chiefly for lending power and thrust to the climax or spreading a rich carpet of sound to accompany string or woodwind solos. The use of the brasses is severely limited by the player's embouchure fatigue. The timbre may be altered by the partial stopping of the "bell" (the large flared end of the instrument) with the hand, a hat, or a mute.

1. TRUMPET. The trumpet is the soprano and the most agile of the brass instruments, its technique permitting rapid repeated notes, quick arpeggios, and (since the invention of valves) fairly rapid scale passages. The principal early use was in playing fanfares and flourishes. The instrument possesses a brilliant and compelling fortissimo.

    SUGGESTED LISTENING—Tchaikovsky: *Italian Caprice*; Beethoven: *Leonore Overture No. 3*; Stravinsky: "Entrance of the Ballerina" from *Petrouchka*.

2. FRENCH HORN. The "horn," as it is called by musicians, is the most expressive of the brass instruments. It possesses a wide range, great dynamic contrast (although lacking the extreme fortissimo of the trumpet), and a quirk of timbre which permits the tone to blend with other brasses or with strings or woodwinds.

SUGGESTED LISTENING—Strauss: *Till Eulenspiegel;* Beethoven: trio of 3rd mvt. of *Symphony No. 3;* Brahms: 1st mvt. of *Piano Concerto No. 2 in B-flat.*

3. TROMBONE. The trombone serves as the tenor and bass of the brasses. The color is darker and more brassy than that of the horn. The pianissimo is mellow and the powerful fortissimo of the instrument makes it invaluable in climaxes. Its rapid passage technique is limited by the clumsiness of the slide. Usually employed for broad and dignified passages, the instrument may also be used for a comical effect called a *glissando* (made by moving the slide while tone is being produced).

SUGGESTED LISTENING—Mozart: "Tuba Mirum" from *Requiem;* Wagner: Overture to *Tannhäuser;* Brahms: 4th mvt. of *Symphony No. 4.*

4. TUBA. The tuba is the double bass of the brasses. The color is dark, rich, and somewhat ponderous in the low register and round and melodious in the high.

SUGGESTED LISTENING—Wagner: beginning of Act II of *Siegfried;* Prelude to *Die Meistersinger;* Strauss: *Also Sprach Zarathustra.*

5. OTHER INSTRUMENTS. Other brass instruments include *cornet,* an instrument so closely resembling the trumpet that many musicians cannot distinguish one from the other aurally; *alto horn* or *mellophone,* an instrument that substitutes for French horn; *baritone horn* or *euphonium,* an instrument of considerable flexibility whose range is an octave above that of the tuba; and *sousaphone,* a marching-band instrument whose range and tone resemble those of the tuba.

III. **Percussion instruments.** A percussion instrument is an object which may be struck by another object to produce a sound.

A. INSTRUMENTS OF DEFINITE PITCH

1. TIMPANI (KETTLEDRUMS). The sound of the timpani, a pointed, intense "thump," is produced by striking with a mallet a calfskin "head" stretched tautly over the top of a large copper bowl. The player may "roll" (rapidly reiterated strokes) at all dynamic levels from a tiny pianissimo to a thundering fortissimo.

SUGGESTED LISTENING—Beethoven: 2nd mvt. of *Symphony No. 9;* Dvořák: 3rd mvt. of *Symphony No. 5;* Hanson: scherzo of *Symphony No. 3.*

2. XYLOPHONE. The xylophone, an arrangement of tuned wooden bars which the player strikes with hard mallets, is usually used to add incisiveness to a lively tune.

SUGGESTED LISTENING—Saint-Saëns: *Danse Macabre.*

3. CHIMES. Chimes, an arrangement of resonating metal tubes, yield a church bell effect when struck with a wooden hammer.

SUGGESTED LISTENING—Berlioz: 5th mvt. of *Symphonie Fantastique.*

4. BELLS. Bells are metal bars struck with hard mallets to produce a clear, metallic, percussive tone. A set of portable bells for marching use is called a "glockenspiel."

SUGGESTED LISTENING—Respighi: "Pines of the Villa Borghese" from *Pines of Rome.*

5. OTHER INSTRUMENTS. Less frequently used percussion instruments of definite pitch include the vibra-harp, marimba, selected Pyrex baking dishes, and so on.

B. INSTRUMENTS OF INDEFINITE PITCH. Among the instruments of indefinite pitch are a myriad of objects and devices. The most frequently used include:

1. TRIANGLE. The triangle is a metal rod bent into the shape of an equilateral triangle. When struck with a small metal "beater" it produces a clear, high, bell-like sound.

SUGGESTED LISTENING—Liszt: scherzo from *Piano Concerto No. 1 in E-flat.*

2. SNARE DRUM. The snare drum is a small drum with taut calfskin heads covering each end and gut strings or wire springs called "snares" kept in contact with one head. The sound is a tight, dry rattle when stroked singly with a stick and an intense and stirring noise when "rolled."

SUGGESTED LISTENING—Stravinsky: "Entrance of the Ballerina" from *Petrouchka.*

3. BASS DRUM. Called "bass" because its sound is a conglomeration of many low pitches, this large drum has calfskin heads covering each end. When struck with a beater (a leather or felt-covered ball on the end of a stick) the drum produces a low, ponderous "boom." The fortissimo can even be heard over the thunder of the timpani.

SUGGESTED LISTENING—Respighi: "Pines of the Appian Way" from *Pines of Rome.*

4. CYMBALS. Cymbals are metal plates usually played in pairs, one being struck against the other. The sound is described as a "crash." The size of the cymbals and the force used determine the character of the sound. A single cymbal may be struck with a drum stick or timpani mallet.

SUGGESTED LISTENING—Tchaikovsky: 4th mvt. of *Symphony No. 4.*

5. OTHER INSTRUMENTS. Less commonly used instruments of indefinite pitch include the tambourine, wood block, cow bell, gong, and castanets, among others.

SUGGESTED LISTENING—Rimsky-Korsakov: *Capriccio Espagnole.*

IV. **Keyboard instruments.** The keyboard instruments possess a bank of keys which the player depresses to activate a mechanism which (1) strikes or plucks a string or other vibrating object, (2) channels compressed air into a reed or "edge-tone" apparatus, or (3) controls an electronic sound source.

A. PIANO (contraction of *pianoforte*). The piano is the most common keyboard instrument. Taut strings are struck by hammers to produce tones.

B. ORGAN. The *pipe organ* is an almost unbelievably complex machine whose mechanism may include means of producing tones resembling those of wind instruments as well as the characteristic quality (*diapason*) of the organ. The *electronic organ* is an instrument more or less successfully imitating the sound of the pipe organ.

C. CELESTA. The pleasant, bright, cheerful tinkle of the celesta is produced by tiny hammers striking metal bars.

SUGGESTED LISTENING—Tchaikovsky: "Dance of the Sugar-Plum Fairy" from *The Nutcracker Suite*.

D. OTHER KEYBOARD INSTRUMENTS. The *harpsichord*, shaped somewhat like a grand piano, but much smaller in size, produces its tones by plucking the strings through a mechanism which is controlled by the keyboard. The distinctive timbre is delicate and slightly metallic. The *calliope* is usually associated with outdoor entertainment, and the *accordion* is usually associated with indoor entertainment.

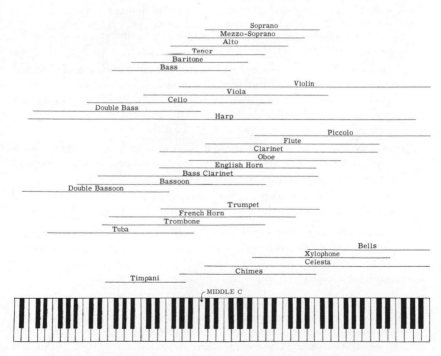

Ranges of voices and instruments compared with piano keyboard.

3

Performance Media

The voice, instrument, or *ensemble* (two or more performers singing or playing together) selected by the composer for the performance of a work is called the "performance medium." A work performed by a medium other than that intended by the composer is called a *transcription*.

I. **Vocal and choral media.** Vocal and choral performances may utilize instrumental accompaniment or may be unaccompanied (*a cappella*).

   A. SOLO VOICE. Most vocal *recitals* (solo performances) today include piano accompaniment.

   B. VOCAL ENSEMBLES. The nomenclature of the various ensembles—*duet, trio, quartet, quintet, sextet,* and so forth—reflects the number of voices used.

   C. CHORAL GROUPS. Choral groups consist of a large number (ten to a multitude) of male, female, or mixed voices.

      1. CHORUS. The term "chorus" is generic for all choral groups. Mixed choruses usually consist of sopranos, altos, tenors, and basses (abbreviated SATB). Women's choruses usually consist of first (high) and second (low) sopranos and altos (SSAA). Men's choruses usually consist of first and second tenors and basses (TTBB).

      2. CHOIR. The term "choir" usually is used in reference to a chorus associated with a church. (It may also be used in connection with groups of instruments analogous to the SATB arrangement of voices.)

      3. A CAPPELLA CHOIR, CONCERT CHOIR, SINGERS, CONCERT CHORALE. These and similar terms are usually associated with collegiate groups.

      4. GLEE CLUB. "Glee club" is the usual designation for collegiate men's or women's choruses.

II. **Instrumental media**

   A. SOLO INSTRUMENT. Certain instruments are better suited to solo performance than others. The greatest quantity of solo literature is for piano or organ, which can perform both tune and accompaniment. Although some literature exists for other instruments unaccompanied (especially violin and cello), most instrumental solos have piano accompaniment.

B. CHAMBER MUSIC ENSEMBLES. In its strictest sense, chamber music refers to music with only one player to each part in contrast to music for larger ensembles with two or more players to the part. Loosely, the term refers to music intended to be performed by a small group in a small hall for a small audience.

1. STRING QUARTET. The string quartet consists of a first violin, second violin, viola, and cello.

2. PIANO TRIO. The piano trio consists of violin, cello, and piano.

3. STRING QUINTET. The string quintet consists of the quartet plus another instrument (often a woodwind).

4. PIANO QUINTET. The piano quintet consists of the quartet of strings plus piano.

5. WOODWIND QUINTET. The woodwind quintet consists of flute, oboe, clarinet, French horn (a *brass* instrument), and bassoon.

6. BRASS QUARTET. The instrumentation of the brass quartet is not standardized. Frequent combinations are: two trumpets and two trombones; two trumpets, horn, and trombone; two trumpets, trombone, and euphonium.

7. PERCUSSION ENSEMBLES. The instrumentation of percussion ensembles varies considerably.

8. KEYBOARD ENSEMBLE. The common ensembles are two players at one or two pianos (the latter called *duo* piano).

C. LARGE ENSEMBLES

1. SYMPHONY ORCHESTRA. The size of the symphony orchestra varies from an amateur group of substandard instrumentation to a professional

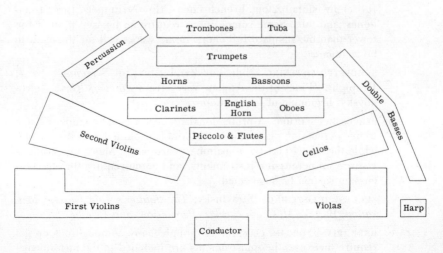

A typical seating plan of a symphony orchestra.

orchestra of more than a hundred players. The size of the orchestra is dependent upon the budget of the supporting agency, no orchestra being self-supporting.

SUGGESTED LISTENING—Britten: *Young Person's Guide to the Orchestra;* Saint-Saëns: *The Carnival of the Animals;* Ravel: *Bolero;* Hanson: *The Composer and His Orchestra.*

a. STRING CHOIR. The orchestra's largest choir contains about two-thirds of the total membership. Capable of great expressiveness, wide pitch and dynamic ranges, and a wealth of color, the string choir is the most versatile. The principal violinist, called the *concertmaster,* was the leader of the orchestra before baton-wielding conductors came into being, and he still ranks as second-in-command. The instrumentation includes ten to eighteen first violins, eight to sixteen second violins, six to fourteen violas, four to twelve cellos, and two to ten double basses.

SUGGESTED LISTENING—Mozart: *Eine Kleine Nachtmusik;* Barber: *Adagio for Strings;* Vaughan Williams: *Fantasia on a Theme of Tallis.*

b. WOODWIND CHOIR. The woodwind choir is the source of much of the vivid tone color in the orchestra. The favorite instrumentations consist of "woodwinds in threes": two flutes and piccolo, two oboes and English horn, two clarinets and bass clarinet, and two bassoons and double bassoon; or "woodwinds in pairs": two each of flutes, oboes, clarinets, and bassoons. Other woodwind instruments may be added if the composer so specifies.

SUGGESTED LISTENING—Mozart: *Serenades for Winds, K. 375, K. 388;* Mendelssohn: scherzo from *A Midsummer Night's Dream;* Tchaikovsky: middle section of 3rd mvt. of *Symphony No. 4.*

c. BRASS CHOIR. The brass choir is small but powerful. The standard full choir contains four French horns, three trumpets, three trombones, and tuba. Some compositions require no brasses at all or use fewer than the standard full choir. Some works call for the choir to be augmented.

SUGGESTED LISTENING—Tchaikovsky: 1st mvt. of *Symphony No. 4;* Respighi: "Pines of the Appian Way" from *Pines of Rome;* Tchaikovsky: beginning of *Italian Caprice.*

d. PERCUSSION SECTION. A professional orchestra usually employs three to five percussion players, one of whom is occupied with the timpani while the others play the remaining instruments. Many compositions require no percussion instruments, and some require that the percussion section be augmented.

SUGGESTED LISTENING—Stravinsky: *The Soldier's Tale;* Varese: *Ionization;* Bartok: *Music for Strings, Percussion, and Celesta.*

e. HARP, PIANO, ORGAN, CELESTA. Although many compositions do not require their use, these instruments are included in the instrumentation of every large orchestra.

2. CHAMBER ORCHESTRA. A chamber orchestra is a small orchestra employing perhaps only a quintet of woodwinds and a quartet of brasses plus
   a small string choir.

3. STRING ORCHESTRA. A string orchestra consists only of the string choir.

4. SYMPHONIC BAND. A symphonic band is a large ensemble of wind and
   percussion instruments, for which there is a growing number of serious
   compositions. The large symphonic band consists of piccolos, flutes,
   oboes, English horns, the entire family of clarinets, bassoons, double
   bassoons, the entire family of saxophones, French horns, trumpets,
   cornets, trombones, baritone horns, tubas, double basses (infrequently),
   and a complete percussion section.

5. SYMPHONIC WIND ENSEMBLE. The symphonic wind ensemble is identical
   in instrumentation to the symphonic band, but employs only one player
   to the part.

part 2

Arrangements in Time

The dimension of time is more important to music than to such arts as painting or sculpture. A line in a statue may be seen in an instant, but a line of melody can be heard only as it unfolds in time. The entire panorama of a painting may be encompassed by a sweeping glance, but the beginning and end of a musical work are separated in time ranging in duration from only two or three minutes for performance of a simple song to more than ten times two or three minutes for a symphony and to several hours for an opera.

Throughout a musical composition, arrangements of sound in time contribute to the feeling that music is in motion. In the composition as a whole, the element of time is essential in conveying a feeling of proportion or balance (or disproportion and imbalance) between the various divisions of the work.

4

Rhythm

Rhythm, growing out of a systematized arrangement of sounds of various duration, is that aspect of music which contributes to the feeling of life and motion in time. The elemental components of rhythm are patterns of sound and silence and a regular rhythmic activity which serves as a background for those patterns.

I. **Patterns of sound and silence.** The materials of rhythm are sound and silence, from which an unlimited number of patterns can be made.

   A. DURATION. Durations of sound and silence are expressed in *notes* and *rests*, respectively. The symbols used in notation indicate relative values of duration.

	Whole	Half	Quarter	Eighth	Sixteenth	Thirty-second
Notes	𝅝	𝅗𝅥	𝅘𝅥	𝅘𝅥𝅮 or	𝅘𝅥𝅯 or	𝅘𝅥𝅰 or
Rests	𝄻	𝄼	𝄽	𝄾	𝄿	𝅀

Successive notes are connected by the <u>tie</u> to sound as one tone.				A dot increases by half the duration of the preceding note or rest.	
written	sound	written	sound	𝅗𝅥. = 𝅗𝅥𝅘𝅥	𝅘𝅥. = 𝅘𝅥𝅘𝅥𝅮

Notation of duration.

   B. ACCENT. An accent occurs when a sound is given greater emphasis than those which surround it. Accents result from longer duration, greater volume, higher pitch, or contrasting timbre.

   C. ARTICULATION. The beginning and end of a sound are called *attack* and *release*, respectively. The performance of attacks and releases is called *articulation*. The use of varying degrees of *staccato* and *legato* articulation is an important factor in interpretation.

21

1. STACCATO. Extreme staccato articulation noticeably detaches notes from each other. The notation usually involves small dots placed directly over or under the notes affected. Sometimes a staccato effect is indicated by a rest following each note or by the written word or its abbreviation "stacc."

SUGGESTED LISTENING—Tchaikovsky: "Dance of the Toy Flutes" from *The Nutcracker Suite*.

2. LEGATO. Extreme legato articulation connects notes without perceptible interruptions between them. The notation may utilize a long curved line called a *slur*, or it may utilize the written word.

SUGGESTED LISTENING—Tchaikovsky: solo for English horn in "Dance of the Toy Flutes" from *The Nutcracker Suite*.

II. **Rhythmic flow.** The term "rhythmic flow" describes the background against which occur notes and rests. As brief intervals of elapsed time are measured by the ticking of a clock, so intervals of elapsed time in music's rhythmic flow are measured by audible or inferred pulses called *beats* and lighter pulses called *offbeats*.

A. TEMPO. Tempo refers to the frequency of the beats. In most compositions a particular tempo is adopted as the established tempo, fluctuations from which are heard as a disturbance of the normal flow. The terminology indicating tempo is usually Italian. The composer may, however, employ equivalent words in his own language.

1. ESTABLISHED TEMPO

   a. ITALIAN TEMPO TERMS. Approximate tempos are usually indicated by Italian words descriptive of walking gaits. The basic terms, which permit considerable difference in interpretation, include: *grave*, very slow; *largo*, slow; *adagio*, moderately slow; *moderato*, moderate tempo (often thought of as being represented by the human pulse rate); *andante*, either slightly slower or slightly faster than moderato, depending upon the interpreter; *allegro*, faster than moderato; *vivace*, fast; *presto*, very fast.

   b. METRONOMIC MARKINGS. Accurate tempo indications include the metronomic marking. A *metronome* is a mechanical device which can be regulated to mark any desired frequency of beats from about forty to about two hundred per minute.

2. FLUCTUATING TEMPO. Fluctuations of tempo are usually indicated by Italian words such as *ritardando*, gradually slowing; *rallentando*, slowing; *accelerando*, gradually accelerating; and *rubato*, unsteady. A return to the established tempo is indicated by the term *a tempo*. If a composition uses more than one tempo, a return to the tempo of the beginning is indicated by the term *tempo primo*.

B. METER. Most watches tick three hundred times per minute. The human ear, seeking always to organize what it hears into comprehensible units, hears the ticks not as evenly accented pulsations, but as groups of pulsations organized by an imagined accent on the first of each group. The ticks may be counted in pairs, in threes, or in larger units which will be perceived as combinations of pairs or threes. The similar grouping, by audible or inferred accents, of the beats and offbeats of the rhythmic flow of music is called *meter*.

Note Value Receiving One Beat	Two Beats per Measure	Three Beats per Measure	Four Beats per Measure	Five Beats per Measure	Six Beats per Measure	Seven Beats per Measure	Nine Beats per Measure	Twelve Beats per Measure
♪	2/8	3/8 in slow tempo	4/8	5/8	6/8 in slow tempo	7/8	9/8 in slow tempo	12/8 in slow tempo
♩	2/4	3/4 in slow tempo	4/4 or C	5/4	6/4 in slow tempo	7/4	9/4 in slow tempo	12/4 in slow tempo
𝅗𝅥	2/2	3/2	4/2	5/2	6/2 (rare)	7/2 (rare)	9/2 (rare)	12/2 (rare)
♩.	6/8 in fast tempo	9/8 in fast tempo	12/8 in fast tempo	15/8 in fast tempo (rare)	The more common signatures are pointed out by dotted-line boxes. At extremely fast tempi, the two, three, and four-beat measures may be conducted one-to-the-bar. At extremely slow tempi, a two-beat bar may be conducted in four, a four-beat bar in eight, and so forth.			
𝅗𝅥.	6/4 in fast tempo	9/4 in fast tempo	12/4 in fast tempo					

Meter signatures.

5

Structure

In verse, metrical feet are combined to form lines, which in turn may be combined in pairs to form couplets, in fours to form quatrains, or in indefinite numbers to form stanzas. Metrical units in music function in the same way, expanding and combining to create structural units of various lengths. The larger structural units may form entire compositions, just as an entire poem may consist of the four lines of a quatrain. As such, these larger units function as musical *forms*, which are discussed in outlines 11 and 12. Their usual function, however, is to serve as internal structural units which are combined to form works of larger dimensions.

I. **Phrase.** A phrase is a unit, often four measures in length, which is terminated by an effect of musical punctuation called a *cadence*.

A cadence can be created by rhythm alone and can occur only when the rhythmic conditions permit it. The degree of finality of a cadence is dependent upon diverse considerations of rhythm, melody, and harmony. A *complete cadence* suggests permanent conclusion; a *half-cadence* suggests temporary cessation of motion. Because phrases of two, four, or eight bars' length are so common, the ear expects cadences at regular intervals, though phrases con-

Phrase, period, double period. "Old Folks at Home."

First 4 bars: phrase.   First 8 bars: period.   All 16 bars: double period.

'Way down up - on de   Swa - nee Ri - ver,   Far, far   a - way,

Dere's where my heart is   turn - ing ev - er, Dere's where de old folks stay.

All   de world is   sad and drear - y,   Ev' - ry where I   roam;

Oh!, dark - ies, how my   heart grows wear - y,   Far from de old folks at home.

taining an odd number of bars, failing to conform to the expected pattern, are by no means uncommon. Such irregular phrases may result from avoiding a cadence by increased rhythmic activity. The cadence of a phrase is *elided* if it is overlapped by the beginning of the next phrase.

II. **Period.** A period is a unit, usually eight bars in length, composed of two phrases. The first phrase, called the *antecedent*, is terminated by a half-cadence. The second, or *consequent*, phrase may be terminated by either kind of cadence.

III. **Double period.** A double period is a unit, usually sixteen bars in length, composed of two periods. Even the shortest musical composition is usually a double period in length.

IV. **Phrase group.** A phrase group is a unit composed of three or more phrases which do not conform to the expected pattern of a double period.

V. **Part.** A part is an internal unit at least a period in length. Parts are usually terminated by strong cadences. The word "part" is also used in its more general sense to designate any internal structural unit.

part 3

Tonal
Organization

Tonal organization refers to all aspects of the relationships of pitch in music. One important aspect of tonal organization is that concerned with the upward and downward motion of successive tones of higher and lower pitch. Successions of notes appear in musical notation from left to right. Thus this organization of successive pitches is often spoken of as the horizontal aspect of music.

A second important aspect of tonal organization has to do with pitches occurring at the same time. Simultaneous tones appear in musical notation one above the other. Thus the organization of simultaneous pitches is often spoken of as the vertical aspect of music.

The use of the words "successive" and "simultaneous" indicate the importance of rhythm to tonal organization. In practice the organization of pitches is always influenced by rhythm. In theory, however, the tonal relationships may be discussed separately.

6

Melody

Melody is created by a succession of pitches, each pitch being heard in relationship to the preceding and following pitches. The texture of music in which melody is influenced only by timbre, rhythm, and pitch is called *monophonic*. Melodies which can be sung are called "vocal melodies"; those presenting considerable difficulty for vocal rendition are called "instrumental melodies."

I. **The pitch spectrum.** Of the multitude of pitches the ear can distinguish, music commonly employs only the eighty-eight which correspond to the eighty-eight keys of the piano. Verbal references to pitch utilize the names of the first seven letters of the alphabet plus the term "sharp" (raising the letter-pitch to the adjacent higher pitch of the same letter name) and the term "flat" (lowering the letter-pitch to the adjacent lower pitch of the same letter name). Seven letters are sufficient since the eighth letter-pitch (octave) so strongly resembles the first that the same letter-name is assigned to it. This octave effect organizes the eighty-eight pitches of the useful spectrum into only twelve different pitches plus their octave duplicates.

II. **Interval relationships.** Each of the twelve different pitches within the octave is separated from its neighbor by an interval called a half-step, two of which form a whole-step. (An interval is the pitch "distance" formed acoustically by the ratio of the vibration frequencies of two tones.) An interval is usually named according to the number of letter-name pitches involved, counting up from the lowest and including both the lowest and the highest pitches.

Intervals above C.

Second   Third   Fourth   Fifth   Sixth   Seventh   Octave

A note may move to another note of different pitch by stepwise (diatonic) movement through the interval of a second, by chromatic movement to a pitch of

29

the same letter-name flatted or sharped, or by leap through an interval larger than a second.

Diatonic progressions.

Chromatic progressions.

III. Melodic contour. The rise and fall of successive pitches of a melody may be visualized as a horizontal line possessing curves, angles, ascending and descending inclines, and plateaus. The conformations of this imaginary line constitute melodic contour.

A. RANGE. The highest and lowest pitches in a contour define its range.

B. TESSITURA. The pitch range within which most of the notes of a contour fall is called the tessitura.

C. CLIMAX. The highest pitch of a contour is called the climax. (The climactic effect is usually reinforced by other elements.)

D. CONTOUR TYPES. The contour type is determined by the intervallic content.

    1. CONJUNCT CONTOUR. A conjunct contour, smooth and curved, results from the use of stepwise and chromatic movement.

    Conjunct melody. "America."

     My coun-try,'tis of thee, Sweet land of li - ber - ty, Of thee I   sing

    2. DISJUNCT CONTOUR. A disjunct contour, jagged and angular, results from the use of many melodic leaps.

    Disjunct melody. "Star-Spangled Banner."

     Oh —   say! can you see, by the   dawn's early   light

IV. Tonality in melody. The notes of most melodies are heard in relationship to each other and also in relationship to a pitch which is felt to be the central pitch. The gravitation toward this central pitch, called the *tonic*, is known as *tonality*. The phenomena of tension and relaxation inherent in tonality governs the shaping of most melodic utterances.

Tonality in melody. "Joy to the World."

Tonic — Tonic — Tonic

Joy to the world! the Lord is come; Let earth re - ceive her king

Pitches may be arranged in artificial ladder-like successions called *scales* or *modes*.

A. SEVEN-TONE SCALES. The common scales contain seven different pitches arranged in order from the tonic to its octave duplicate. This results in the presence of eight scale steps, the tonic being numbered "one" and "eight."

   1. MAJOR SCALES. Major scales coincide with the pattern of whole- and half-steps formed by the letter-name pitches from C to its octave.

   The intervals E–F (steps 3 and 4) and B–C (steps 7 and 8) are half-steps. The remaining intervals between adjacent notes are whole-steps. The intervallic pattern of the major scale is the standard with which other scales are compared.

   Major scale.

   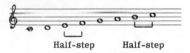

   Half-step   Half-step

   2. MINOR SCALES. A half-step between the second and third scale steps characterizes the several forms of the minor scales. The interval between the fifth and sixth steps and that between the seventh and eighth steps may be either a half-step or a whole-step.

   Minor scale.

   Half-step

   3. ARCHAIC MODAL SCALES. Many melodies are based upon archaic scales called *modes*, most of which are characterized by a whole-step between the seventh scale-step and the tonic.

   Modal scale.

   Whole step

B. PENTATONIC SCALE. Many melodies are based on a gapped scale of five tones, called a pentatonic scale.

Pentatonic scale.

C. WHOLE-TONE SCALE. Many exotic melodies are based on a six-tone scale in which all adjacent steps are a whole-step apart.

Whole-tone scale.

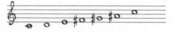

D. TWELVE-TONE SCALES. A twelve-tone scale contains all the pitches between a note and its octave.

1. TONAL USE. A twelve-tone scale, each tone of which is related to the tonic, is called a *chromatic scale.*

Chromatic scale.

2. ATONAL USE. A special technique of melody writing in *tone rows* creates an effect called "atonality" (without tonality). The row consists of a melody containing all the twelve tones with the repetition of a tone avoided until all twelve have been stated, lest a tone gain by its repetition some greater significance than the others.

Tone row. Schoenberg, *Quintet for Wind Instruments, Op. 26.*

Copyright 1925 by Universal Edition, Vienna, renewed 1952 by Gertrud Schoenberg; used by permission of Associated Music Publishers, Inc., New York.

E. ARBITRARY SCALES. Melodies in some modern works are based on scales which do not conform to standard patterns.

F. SCALES CONTAINING MICROTONES. Some modern works use intervals smaller than a half-step, called microtones. Most such works require the use of specially constructed musical instruments.

7

Counterpoint

The general term *counterpoint* refers to the simultaneous occurrence of two or more melodies, one of which may be a *subject* with which countermelodies (also called counterpoints) coexist. The texture of *contrapuntal* music is described as *polyphonic*.

I. **Horizontal aspect.** The principal interest in counterpoint lies in the horizontal activity of the simultaneous melodies and in the degree of their mutual independence of rhythm and of contour.

Two-voice counterpoint. Dvorak: *Symphony No. 5*, 1st movement.

II. **Vertical aspect.** An important secondary interest in counterpoint lies in the intervallic relationships between the simultaneous melodic lines.

A. INTERVAL NOMENCLATURE. The unison, the octave, and the intervals between the tonic of major and minor scales and their fourth and fifth steps are called *perfect* intervals. The intervals between the tonic of a major scale and its second, third, sixth, and seventh steps are called *major*. Intervals one-half step smaller than major are called *minor*. Intervals one-half step larger than perfect or major are called *augmented;* those one-half step smaller than perfect or minor are called *diminished*.

B. INTERVAL QUALITY. Vertical intervals are described as *consonant*, in agreement or accord, or *dissonant*, in disagreement or discord.

1. CONSONANT INTERVALS. Most listeners interpret as consonant all perfect intervals, major and minor thirds, and major and minor sixths.

Consonant intervals above C.

BRIAR CLIFF COLLEGE
LIBRARY
SIOUX CITY, IOWA

32321

2. DISSONANT INTERVALS. Most listeners interpret as dissonant major and minor seconds, major and minor sevenths, augmented fourths, and diminished fifths.

Dissonant intervals above C.

a. CONTROLLED DISSONANCE. Much of the dissonance in music is contrapuntally controlled, the dissonance being surrounded by consonance in such a way that the listener anticipates the clash, hears it occur, and then hears it resolve to consonance.

Two devices for dissonance control.

b. FREE DISSONANCE. In so-called linear counterpoint, in which activity of the simultaneous melodies is all-important, dissonance control is abandoned and consecutive clashes occur freely.

III. Diagonal aspect. To the vertical and horizontal interests in counterpoint, a diagonal interest is added by *imitation* (see outline 10).

8

Harmony

Harmony is concerned with *chords* and their progressions.

I. **Chords.** Three or more pitches sounded together form a chord. In incomplete chords some of the pitches are implied rather than sounded. In *arpeggios,* or "broken chords," the pitches are sounded in close succession rather than simultaneously. The texture of music in which a melody is accompanied by chords is called *homophonic.*

    A. TERTIAN HARMONY. In tertian harmony, chords are erected in thirds above a fundamental pitch called a *root.*

        1. TRIADS. A triad is a three-tone tertian chord. Because much music employs four-part harmony (SATB) one member of a triad is often sounded in two voices.

        CEG triad.

        2. TRIADS WITH ADDED TONES. For increased tension and complexity, other tones may be added to triads, particularly those tones lying a sixth, seventh, ninth, and thirteenth above the root of the triad.

        CEGB♭ 7th chord.

        3. POLYCHORDS. Two or more triads sounded together form a polychord.

        Polychord. B♭DF plus FAC.

B. NON-TERTIAN HARMONY. In non-tertian harmony the erection of chords is based on an interval other than the third.

   1. QUARTAL HARMONY. In quartal harmony chords are erected in fourths.

   Quartal chord.

   2. CHORDS DERIVED FROM ARBITRARY SCALES. The chords used in works based on arbitrary scales or tone rows may resemble tertian chords but are usually of greater complexity.

   3. TONE CLUSTERS. A tone cluster is an extraordinarily complex sonority occurring primarily in piano music. The player is directed to depress several adjacent keys with his fist or forearm.

C. CONSONANCE AND DISSONANCE. The degree of dissonance of a chord is determined by the number of dissonant intervals it contains. The tension and relaxation of dissonance is an important factor in harmonic progression (the effect created by moving from chord to successive chord).

Most listeners interpret the degree of dissonance of chords as follows: least dissonant—triads; more dissonant—triads with added tones; most dissonant—polychords, chords derived from artificial scales, and tone clusters.

Increasing dissonance.

II. Tonality.
The phenomenon of tonality in harmony is closely related to tonality in melody. The triad erected on the *tonic* note is called the *tonic chord,* and the other chords in the key tend to resolve toward that tonic.

A. MAJOR KEYS. In major keys the chords are drawn basically from the major scale.

Triads in key of C Major.

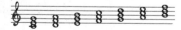

B. MINOR KEYS. In minor keys the chords are drawn from the several forms of the minor scale.

Triads in key of C Minor.

C. MODULATION. Modulation is the process of changing from one key to another.

part 4

Ideas
in Music

The composition of a musical work is inspired by one or more ideas to be expressed in sound.

Sometimes the idea concerns something outside the music such as a person, place, thing, or concept of literary, historical, nationalistic, geographic, racial, religious, emotional, or naturalistic character. Such an extramusical idea is called a *program* and the music inspired by it *program music*. Extramusical ideas in program music are usually pointed out in the title and are sometimes delineated in a program note appended to the score.

Absolute music, on the other hand, is inspired by ideas concerning the organization of musical materials as such, interesting and enjoyable for their own sake. The titles of absolute works are in musical terms which indicate or imply such factors as tempo, tonality, general style, and performance medium.

9
Presentation

I. Musical ideas. In both program music and absolute music, musical ideas are presented as organizations of sound, usually as patterns of rhythm and melody. They may, however, be presented as particular effects of timbre, striking harmonic sonorities or progressions, relationships between tonalities, or other abstract manipulations of musical material.

   A. MOTIVE. A motive is a simple musical idea, sometimes consisting of as few as two notes. A motive may owe its striking and memorable quality to its rhythmic pattern or to its melodic configuration.

   Rhythmic motive. Beethoven: *Symphony No. 5,* 1st movement.

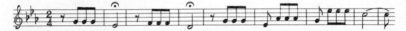

   B. SUBJECT. A subject is a complex musical idea expressed as a prominent melody. A subject is always a tune, but a tune is a subject only if it is used as a component of a longer and more complex work. Subjects, also called *themes,* and their constituent motives are referred to as *thematic material.*

II. Extramusical ideas. The most obvious expression of an extramusical idea is a sung or spoken text. Extramusical ideas can also be represented in program music by devices ranging from realistic sound effects to tenuous psychological associations of moods with musical effects.

   A. REPRODUCTION OF SOUNDS. Extramusical ideas are realistically projected by reproduction of sounds, some scores calling for the use of sound effects such as actual locomotive and boat whistles, automobile horns, firearms, and recordings of birdsongs.

   B. IMITATION OF SOUNDS. The program may be reflected by imitation of sounds such as thunder, wind, rain, birdsongs, battle, running water, automobile horns, breaking glass, falling objects, and animal cries.

C. IMITATION OF MOVEMENTS. The direction of a melodic line may represent ascending or descending movements. Effects of harmony, counterpoint, or dynamics may convey the idea of expanding, contracting, approaching, retreating, materializing, and vanishing. Rhythm may imitate such motions as hesitation, running, stopping, stumbling, marching, and dancing.

D. PORTRAYAL OF EMOTION. Emotional states such as excitement, serenity, anxiety, anguish, joy, sorrow, confidence, exultation, and resignation may be represented by psychologically associated musical effects.

E. LEITMOTIV. A leitmotiv (leading motive) is a motive intended to represent a person, place, thing, or concept which has special significance in the musical composition.

10

Expansion

Musical ideas are usually expanded by immediate recurrence in identical or more or less similar form or by recurrence after a digression to other ideas.

I. **Repetition.** The most common means of recurrence is repetition. Many children's songs and primitive chants consist primarily of repetitions of a short motive.

Melodic repetition. "Silent Night."

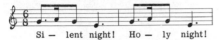

II. **Imitation.** A subject stated in one voice may be imitated in another voice. The recurrence of the subject is called the *answer.*

A. REAL ANSWER. If the contour of the answer is an exact duplicate of that of the subject (even though it may begin at a different pitch) it is called a real answer.

Real answer. Bach: *Fugue in C Major* **from the** *Well-Tempered Clavichord,* *Vol. I, No. 1.*

B. TONAL ANSWER. In the tonal answer the basic shape of the contour is maintained while one or more of the intervals are altered.

Tonal answer. Bach: *Fugue in C Minor* **from the** *Well-Tempered Clavichord,* *Vol. I, No. 2.*

41

C. STRETTO. If the answer begins before the subject is concluded an overlapping effect called stretto results.

Stretto. Bach: *Fugue in C Major* **from the** *Well-Tempered Clavichord,* *Vol. I, No. 1.*

Answer in stretto

D. CANON. Continuous imitation in which the subject is several phrases long and a real answer occurs in stretto is called canon. The most familiar form of canon is the *round* in which, after stating the entire tune, each voice returns immediately to the beginning and repeats it.

Two-voice canon. Franck: *Sonata in A Major for Violin and Piano,* **4th movement.**

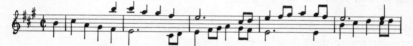

III. **Variation.** Musical subjects, especially themes, may be varied by altering certain characteristics and retaining others.

A. TONE COLOR. With different instrumentation, a subject may recur with new tone color, other elements remaining unchanged.

B. RHYTHM. A subject may be varied in recurrence by use of different rhythm.

1. AUGMENTATION. Augmentation occurs when the duration of each note and rest is longer (usually doubled) than that of the original.

Augmentation. Bach: *Fugue in E Flat Minor* **from the** *Well-Tempered Clavichord, Vol. I, No. 8.*

Subject in augmentation

2. DIMINUTION. A diminution occurs when the duration of each note is shorter (usually halved) than the original.

Diminution. Dvořák: *Symphony No. 5*, 4th movement.

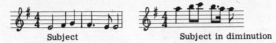

Subject   Subject in diminution

3. OTHER RHYTHMIC ALTERATIONS. Other variations in rhythm include changes in tempo, meter, and rhythmic pattern.

C. MELODY. Alterations of the melodic contour of a subject may take place while other features remain unchanged.

1. SEQUENCE. A sequence occurs when the same contour sounds at a different pitch level.

Sequence. "America."

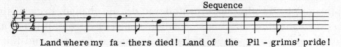

Land where my fa - thers died! Land of   the   Pil - grims' pride!

2. EMBELLISHMENT. Embellishment occurs when the important notes of a contour are ornamented with unessential notes.

Ornamented melody. Haydn: *Symphony No. 94*, 2nd movement.

Ornamentation

D. COUNTERPOINT. In addition to employing the devices of imitation, the variation of a subject may introduce countermelodies.

Countermelody. Haydn: *Symphony No. 94*, 2nd movement.

E. HARMONY. Harmonic alterations may include transposition to different keys and the use of new chords or different progressions.

Variation in harmony. Haydn: *Symphony No. 94*, 2nd movement.

Theme in original harmony

Varied harmony

IV. Transformation. Transformation is a technique which tends to conceal the connection between a subject and its recurrent form. A transformation occurs when one characteristic feature of a motive or theme is retained (not necessarily duplicated) while other features undergo drastic change. Because the distinction between variation and transformation is one of degree, it is not always possible to pinpoint where one of these techniques is dropped and the other is begun.

Transformation of theme. Liszt: *Les Preludes*.

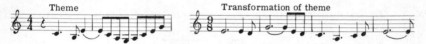

In many compositions all the themes are related to a germinal motive by transformation. It is often difficult to determine whether a subject is new or a transformation of an old one. Subjects may be successively transformed to such a degree that the last theme may seem to have no relationship at all to the original one.

V. Development. The techniques of development include all the devices of imitation, variation, and transformation, the thematic materials being manipulated in such a way as to create a feeling of growing intensity. The themes may be fragmented into constituent motives, motives may be stated in different keys in rapid succession, and two or more melodic fragments may be presented simultaneously.

part 5

Forms
and Types

As a musical work is performed, the perceptive listener hears, in addition to momentary detail, such things as the proportions of the structural units, the order of presentation of motives and subjects, the expansion and derivation of musical ideas, and the relationship of the parts to the whole.

In many works these matters of proportion, order, expansion, derivation, and relationship are arranged in accordance with the scheme of one or another of the musical *forms*. The traditional forms are aesthetically satisfactory designs to which some works adhere exactly, some only in principle, and others not at all.

Compositions which do not conform to specific structural arrangements may be classified as examples of *types*, in which characteristics of general style, dimension, and performance medium may be expected, but in which no specific form is presupposed.

Although all music is conveniently classified here as "instrumental" or "vocal," the categories are not mutually exclusive. Many works which are primarily instrumental use voices, and most vocal works use accompanying instruments.

11

Instrumental Music

Instrumental music does not require singers. However, incidental vocal sections occur in some instrumental works.

I. **Single movement forms.** A movement is a complete musical composition combined with related movements into a larger work. There are often passages from which thematic material is absent: an *introduction* may occur before the theme is stated; *transitions* (called *episodes* in contrapuntal works) may occur between statements or expansions of themes; and a *coda* (tail) may occur after the final statement or expansion of a theme.

   A. PART FORMS. In the part forms similar and contrasting parts or sections are juxtaposed. In discussing internal thematic organization, the letter "A" is often used to represent each appearance of the first theme, with successive letters of the alphabet representing successive themes. A variant of a previously introduced theme is indicated by the letter representing that theme plus a superscript number. Capital letters are usually employed to represent major structural units while lower-case letters may be used for smaller units.

   1. BINARY (TWO-PART) FORM. Binary form consists of a unified whole divided into two complementary parts and separated by a complete cadence. Either or both parts may be repeated. The form is diagrammed AB if the second part is significantly different from the first, or AA¹ if the thematic material of the second part is closely akin to that of the first.

   The second part often consists of thematic material from the first part inverted, fragmented, and sequenced in various keys. A binary form of modest dimensions is sometimes called a *two-part song form.*

   LINE SCORES—Bach: Sarabande, Bourrée I, Bourrée II, Polonaise, "double" of the Polonaise, Minuet, and Badinerie from *Suite No. 2 in B Minor.*

   2. TERNARY (THREE-PART) FORM. The aesthetic principle of return after contrast governs the structure of ternary form, which consists of three parts, the statement of a first or *principal* theme, the statement of a second or *subordinate* contrasting theme, and a restatement of the principal theme. The form is diagrammed ABA.

   A ternary form of special importance is the *song form and trio,* in

47

which each of the three parts is itself a small binary or ternary song form. The typical form is diagrammed:

A	B	A
(aababa)	(ccdcdc)	(aba)

In early examples of the form the B section is scored for only three instrumental parts, hence the name *trio*. In the tradition so established, the B section usually employs fewer instruments than are used in the A section.

LINE SCORES—Beethoven: 3rd mvt. of *Symphony No. 5;* Dvořák: 2nd mvt. of *Symphony No. 5;* Mozart: 3rd mvt. of *Eine Kleine Nachtmusik.* ANALYSES—Chopin: *Etude in E, Op. 10, No. 3;* Mendelssohn: 2nd mvt. of *Violin Concerto in E Minor;* Schoenberg: 3rd mvt. of *Quintet for Wind Instruments, Op. 26;* Schumann: 2nd mvt. of *Piano Concerto in A Minor.*

3. RONDO FORM. The rondo form consists of statements, restatements, variants, or abbreviations of the first theme (sometimes called the rondo theme) alternated with statements of new themes. The simplest rondo is diagrammed ABACA.

Longer rondos may employ four themes, arranged ABACADA. Modifications of the rondo principle may result in forms diagrammed ABACABA and ABCBA. Sometimes in these modified forms the C section is a development of the principal theme.

LINE SCORES—Bach: rondeau from *Suite No. 2 in B Minor;* Dvořák: 3rd mvt. of *Symphony No. 5.* ANALYSES—Beethoven: 2nd and 3rd mvts. of *Piano Sonata No. 8 in C Minor ("Pathétique");* Schoenberg: 4th mvt. of *Quintet for Wind Instruments, Op. 26.*

SUGGESTED LISTENING—Beethoven: 3rd mvt. of *Concerto in D for Violin;* Haydn: 4th mvt. of *Symphony No. 97,* 4th mvt. of *Symphony No. 101;* Saint-Saëns: *Introduction and Rondo Capriccioso.*

B. VARIATION FORMS. The variation of a musical idea is by no means applied only in the variation forms. In these forms, however, variation techniques dominate the musical fabric.

1. THEME AND VARIATIONS. This form consists of the statement of a theme followed by variations on that theme. The number of variations and the treatment of each variation are arbitrarily determined by the composer. In many works each variation assumes a specific character, as of a march or dance. Though most works in this form are based on a single theme, some works treat two themes in variation. A few composers have introduced the theme after the variations instead of before.

LINE SCORES—Beethoven: 2nd mvt. of *Symphony No. 5;* Haydn: 2nd mvt. of *Symphony No. 94.* ANALYSES—Rachmaninoff: *Rhapsody on a Theme of Paganini.*

SUGGESTED LISTENING—Beethoven: 4th mvt. of *Symphony No. 3;* Britten:

Young Person's Guide to the Orchestra; Elgar: *Enigma Variations;* Schubert: 4th mvt. of *Piano Quintet in A Major ("Trout").*

2. PASSACAGLIA AND CHACONNE. In the passacaglia a theme presented in the bass voice recurs with little or no modification while new melodic ideas occur in the upper voices. The chaconne is closely akin to the passacaglia, the distinction being that the chord progression remains intact in the chaconne while melody, timbre, and rhythm are varied. A work in which the theme is only a phrase long is called a *basso ostinato* or *ground.*

LINE SCORES—Purcell: "Dido's Lament" from *Dido and Aeneas.* ANALYSES—Bach: *Passacaglia in C Minor.*

SUGGESTED LISTENING—Bach: chaconne from *Partita in D Minor for Violin, Unaccompanied,* "Crucifixus" from *Mass in B Minor;* Brahms: 4th mvt. of *Symphony No. 4.*

3. CHORALE PRELUDE. A chorale prelude is a contrapuntal composition, usually for organ, based upon the tune of a chorale. The subject may appear in long notes, usually in the bass or soprano; highly embellished in the soprano; in contrapuntal imitation in all voices; or in combinations of these.

C. FUGAL FORMS. The imitation of a subject (sometimes called "fugal treatment") is by no means restricted to the fugal forms. In these forms, however, the application of imitation techniques dominates the entire fabric.

1. FUGUE. The fugue is the most complex and ambitious form of imitation. If the answer is real the fugue is called "real." If the answer is tonal the fugue is called "tonal." Fugues also occur in choral music. A fugue consists of: *expositions,* which employ most of the devices of contrapuntal imitation while the subject or answer appears at least once in each voice (although sometimes expositions are incomplete), and *episodes,* which do not employ the subject in its entirety. The contours and rhythms of voices which are not involved in statements of the subject or answer usually reflect important motives taken from the subject or the accompanying counterpoint. A *double fugue* is based on two subjects. A *fughetta* is a diminutive fugue of only one exposition.

LINE SCORES—Bach: *Fugue No. 2, Well-Tempered Clavichord, Volume I.* ANALYSES—Bach: *Fugue No. 1, Well-Tempered Clavichord, Volume I.*

2. INVENTION. An invention is a keyboard composition closely akin to the fugue but without refined devices such as augmentation and diminution. *Real answers* predominate.

D. DEVELOPMENT FORMS. The use of thematic development is not at all limited to the development forms. In these forms, however, the technique assumes special importance.

1. SONATA-ALLEGRO FORM (sometimes called "sonata form" or "first movement form"). The most sophisticated single movement form consists typically of three sections: the statement of two contrasting thematic

ideas, the development of those ideas, and the restatement of those ideas.

INTRODUCTION. If an introduction begins the movement, the tempo will usually be slow regardless of the tempo of the movement proper. The introduction is often thematically unrelated to the remainder.

EXPOSITION. The *first theme group* consists of statements of one or more themes with extensions or modifications of the themes. The first theme group is unified by style and by tonality, the themes being announced in the key of the movement. The *transition* is usually based thematically on developmental treatment of the material of the first theme group and "bridges" and modulates from the first group to the second group. The *second theme group* contrasts with the first group, frequently being more lyric and in a contrasting key.

DEVELOPMENT. In the development section (sometimes called the "fantasia section"), unfettered by any restrictions of form, any or all of the themes are developed and "worked out." New thematic material is rarely introduced since composers take great pride in "sticking to the text."

RECAPITULATION. The recapitulation is a modified re-statement of the exposition. The first theme group is sometimes abbreviated. The transition is so modified that it remains in the key of the movement. The second theme group occurs here in the same key as that of the first group.

CODA. The coda may be a brief closing section, or it may approach the dimension and content of another development section. New material is sometimes introduced.

LINE SCORES—Beethoven: 1st and 4th mvts. of *Symphony No. 5;* Brahms: 1st mvt. of *Sonata in D Minor for Violin and Piano;* Dvořák: 1st and 4th mvts. of *Symphony No. 5;* Mozart: 4th mvt. of *Eine Kleine Nachtmusik.* ANALYSES—Beethoven: 1st mvt. of *Piano Sonata No. 8 in C Minor ("Pathétique");* Mendelssohn: 1st mvt. of *Violin Concerto in E Minor;* Schumann: 1st and 3rd mvts. of *Piano Concerto in A Minor;* Tchaikovsky: *Romeo and Juliet.*

2. SONATINA FORM (ABRIDGED SONATA-ALLEGRO FORM). Sonatina form is distinguished from sonata-allegro form chiefly by the abbreviation or the absence of a development section. In those works lacking a development section the techniques of development are employed in the transitions and in the coda.

LINE SCORES—Mozart: 1st mvt. of *Eine Kleine Nachtmusik;* Brahms: 2nd mvt. of *Sonata in D Minor for Violin and Piano.*

SUGGESTED LISTENING—Franck: 1st mvt. of *Sonata for Violin and Piano;* Mozart: 2nd mvt. of *String Quartet in C Major, K. 465;* Schubert: 2nd mvt. of *Symphony No. 8.*

E. FREE FORMS. In the free forms no specific arrangement of thematic material may be expected. The structures may be identical with those discussed above, or they may consist of a number of sections held together by similarities of style, harmonic treatment, and rhythmic usage. Structures in which a number of themes are presented in a free order are called "episodic."

1. PRELUDE. A prelude is an episodic work which may be independent or prefatory to a musico-dramatic work.

2. OVERTURE. An overture is usually a work prefacing a stage production, but it may exist as an independent composition.

   a. PREFATORY OVERTURE. An overture to a dramatic production may use thematic material from the work which follows. The structure often is sonata-allegro. A prefatory overture introducing several themes episodically is called a *potpourri overture*.

   b. CONCERT OVERTURE. An independent work, usually programmatic, the concert overture may be episodic or in sonata-allegro form.

   LINE SCORES—Bach: Overture from *Suite No. 2 in B Minor;* Wagner: Overture to *Tannhäuser*. ANALYSES—Tchaikovsky: *Romeo and Juliet.*

3. FANTASIA. A fantasia is an episodic work in the character of a written-out improvisation. (An improvisation is an extemporaneous creative performance, usually on a keyboard instrument.)

4. SINFONIA. A sinfonia is a brief instrumental movement prefatory to a choral composition.

   ANALYSES—Bach: sinfonia of *Cantata No. 4, "Christ Lag in Todesbanden."*

5. CHARACTER PIECE. A character piece is a work expressing a mood, an emotion, or a concept. In many the fanciful title is the only program matic element. The design is often ternary.

   Among the various titles used are: *Album Leaves, Arabesque, Bagatelle, Ballade, Capriccio, Carnaval, Etude, Impromptu, Intermezzo, Moment Musicale, Nocturne, Novelette, Serenade, Song Without Words,* and *Waltz.*

   ANALYSES—Chopin: *Etude in E, Op. 10, No. 3.*

6. RHAPSODY. A rhapsody is an episodic work of pretentious dimensions. The term is sometimes applied to an enthusiastic set of variations on a (frequently nationalistic) theme.

   ANALYSES—Rachmaninoff: *Rhapsody on a Theme of Paganini.*

7. TONE POEM (SYMPHONIC POEM). A tone poem is a programmatic composition of large proportions. The program, usually nationalistic, epic, or heroic, is suggested by the title and is sometimes set forth in a "program note" appended to the score.

   A program of a dramatic nature is frequently unfolded in sonata-allegro form, conflict being depicted by the clash of the themes in the development section. Other situations are expressed in ternary, rondo, or episodic autogenetic (self-generating) structures related by thematic transformations of a germinal motive.

ANALYSES—Debussy: *Prelude to the Afternoon of a Faun;* Liszt: *Les Preludes;* Respighi: *Pines of Rome;* Smetana: *The Moldau.*

II. Composite forms. Composite works (with a few conspicuous exceptions) consist of two or more movements often related to each other by subtle thematic similarities. If the thematic relationship is obvious, the work is called *cyclic.*

A. WORKS IN THE FORM OF THE SONATA. The sonata form, employed for the most pretentious and serious works in absolute music, usually consists of three or four movements. The term "sonata" is also used in its original sense of the Italian verb *sonare* (to sound), thus distinguishing an instrumental work from a vocal work, the latter being called *cantata,* from the Italian *cantare* (to sing).

The first movement, with rare exceptions, is a moderately fast movement in sonata-allegro form.

The second movement is usually a slow movement of lyric quality. The tonality usually contrasts with the key of the work as a whole. The form may be one of the part forms, one of the sectional-contrast forms, sonata-allegro, a sonatina form, or a theme and variations.

The third movement (of four movement works) is usually a dance-like or buoyant movement in ternary form. The tonality usually contrasts with the key of the work as a whole and the meter is usually triple.

The last movement is usually a fast or triumphant finale. The tonality usually conforms to that of the composition as a whole. The form is frequently a rondo, sometimes a theme and variations, a sonata-allegro, or a sonatina.

Three-movement works omit the dance-like movement. A work of five movements usually has an additional slow movement inserted between the dance-like movement and the finale. The movements sometimes are designed to be performed without pause between them, the demarcation being apparent in the sudden tempo change involved. Sometimes the dance-like movement precedes the slow movement.

1. SONATA. The sonata is the work for solo instrument with piano or for piano alone which gave its name to the form. There are usually three movements. Violin and cello are the favored solo instruments.

LINE SCORES—Brahms: *Sonata in D Minor for Violin and Piano.* ANALYSES—Beethoven: *Piano Sonata No. 8 in C Minor ("Pathétique").*

2. CONCERTO. A work for solo instrument with orchestra is called a concerto. There are usually three movements.

Two striking features of the concerto are the first movement's double exposition (the themes announced separately by the orchestra and the solo instrument) and the *cadenza,* an unaccompanied rhapsodic virtuoso passage based on motives from the themes.

ANALYSES—Mendelssohn: *Violin Concerto in E Minor;* Schumann: *Piano Concerto in A Minor.*

3. SYMPHONY. The symphony is a work for orchestra. There are usually four movements. A symphony with a program is called a *programmatic symphony.* A diminutive symphony is called a *sinfonietta.*

LINE SCORES—Beethoven: *Symphony No. 5;* Dvořák: *Symphony No. 5.*

4. CHAMBER ENSEMBLE. A work for chamber ensemble is usually in four movements. The standard group is the string quartet. Others include string trio, piano trio, string quintet, piano quintet, and quartet of strings plus a wind instrument.

ANALYSES—Schoenberg: *Quintet for Wind Instruments, Op. 26.*

B. SONATINA. Instrumental solos of smaller dimension and less profound character than sonatas are often cast in a composite structure whose first movement is in sonatina form. There are ordinarily two and seldom more than three movements. The last movement is usually a spirited rondo.

C. TRIO SONATA. A trio sonata is a work for four instruments (usually two violins, cello, and keyboard) which play only three parts, the cello duplicating the bass line of the keyboard instrument. The *sonata da chiesa,* intended for performance in church, usually consists of four binary movements arranged Slow—Fast—Slow—Fast. The *sonata da camera,* intended for performance in secular surroundings, resembles the dance suite.

D. CONCERTO GROSSO. A concerto grosso is a work usually in three binary movements (Fast—Slow—Fast) in which are contrasted a small group of instruments called the *concertino* (usually the same instruments employed in the trio sonata) with a larger string group called the *ripieno.*

E. BALLET. A ballet is an art form combining the elements of music with those of the dance. The music and the choreography (routine of steps, motions, postures, and so forth) unite in conveying the program. Much ballet music is of sufficient intrinsic interest for concert performance.

F. INCIDENTAL MUSIC. Incidental music is intended to accompany the performance of a play. Such works may contain overtures, entr'acte music (to be played between acts), and "background music" to establish mood and to accompany the business on stage.

G. SUITE. A multi-movement composition lacking the formal organization of the sonata or sonatina may be called a suite.

1. DANCE SUITE. The dance suite is a work in four to eight movements which are named according to the dance style of the music. Dance suites are also called *partitas* or *sonata-suites.* The movements are frequently ordered: *allemande,* in moderate tempo, quadruple meter; *courante,* in moderate tempo, triple meter; *sarabande,* in slow tempo, triple meter; *minuet,* in moderate tempo, triple meter; and *gigue,* in fast tempo, duple meter.

LINE SCORES—Bach: *Suite No. 2 in B Minor.*

2. DIVERTIMENTO. A divertimento is a suite of light and entertaining character in four to ten movements. Divertimentos are also called *cassations* or *serenades.* The multi-movement serenade should not be confused with the single movement character piece entitled "Serenade."

LINE SCORES—Mozart: *Eine Kleine Nachtmusik.*

3. SUITE OF INCIDENTAL MUSIC. Incidental music is often presented in concert arranged as a suite.

4. OPERA AND BALLET SUITE. Music from an opera, a ballet, or musical comedy is often presented in concert arranged as a suite.

ANALYSES—Copland: *Billy the Kid;* Stravinsky: *Petrouchka.*

5. SYMPHONIC SUITE. The symphonic suite is independent of theatrical origin or association with dancing, but frequently is of programmatic inspiration.

12

Vocal Music

The text usually determines the form of a vocal work. Instruments are employed merely for accompaniment or for incidental purposes. Prose texts suggest unmetrical settings. Poetry suggests metrical settings and the re-use of thematic material by couplets and stanzas in AB or ABA arrangements.

A *strophic* form results if each poetic stanza is set to the same music. A *modified strophic* form results if each stanza is set to music essentially the same but differing in detail. If each stanza is given a different musical setting, the work is "through-composed" (*durchkomponiert*).

I. **Single number forms.** The single number forms constitute relatively short, complete, individual compositions which may be combined with other "numbers" and with instrumental movements to form composite works.

    A. RECITATIVE. Imitating the inflections and rhythms of speech, recitatives present narrative or descriptive detail in succinct form. The design is usually through-composed. Recitatives are *secco* (dry) if the accompaniment is minimal, or "accompanied" if the instrumental support is elaborate.

    B. PLAINSONG OR PLAINCHANT. Plainsong refers to unmetrical monophonic compositions, the most important of which are Gregorian chants, settings of the liturgy of the Roman Catholic Church. Recurring textual portions of the liturgy are often set to the same music, creating some formal organization by repetition. The melodic intervals are small, the range severely restricted, the contour smooth, and the rhythm unhurried and free, devoid of heavy accent.

    LINE SCORES—Gregorian chant (selections).

    C. SONG. A song is a lyric setting of a poetic text intended for solo voice and sung with or without accompaniment. The term is also used in connection with instrumental compositions of a song-like nature or with instrumental renditions of transcribed vocal music.

        1. FOLK SONG. Folk songs are lyrical expressions descriptive of the life, customs, and spirit of a society.

55

a. "TRUE" FOLK SONG. A "true" folk song is a work of one or more improvisors whose identity has been lost in time while the song has been transmitted (usually with modifications) from singer to singer.

b. COMPOSED FOLK SONG. A composed folk song is a song of considerable longevity and popularity, the composer of which is known.

2. ART SONG. The art song, called *lied* in German (plural form, *lieder*) and *chanson* in French, is a composed song which, ideally, achieves a perfect matching of the music and the text. The melody and the accompaniment usually reflect the meaning of the text by devices of *text-painting* (imitating sounds, movements, and so forth). The careful connection of the text with the music results in the usual modified strophic or through-composed settings.

LINE SCORES—Schubert: *Der Erlkönig, Der Wanderer.*

3. ARIA. An aria is an elaborate, accompanied song in which the music dominates the text and (it has been said) the singer dominates the music. Most arias occur as numbers in composite works, the aria commenting or reflecting upon the situation established in a preceding recitative. The structure of an aria usually consists of three sections, the last returning to the theme after the digression of the middle section. An independent, virtuoso solo song is sometimes called a *concert aria.* An *arioso* is an accompanied, song-like recitative. An *arietta* is a diminutive and less ambitious aria.

LINE SCORES—arias from Handel: *Messiah* and Mozart: *The Marriage of Figaro.*

D. HYMN. Hymns are simple metrical settings of brief religious or patriotic texts suitable for singing by untrained voices. The pitch range is restricted, the rhythm simple, and the melody conjunct. Each stanza of the strophic setting often consists of a double period.

E. CHORALE. The hymn of the German Lutheran Church is called a chorale. Originally intended for congregational singing with organ accompaniment, chorales are now usually performed in SATB harmonization, often as parts of larger works. The range is restricted and the rhythm simple, the quarter note in 4/4 meter prevailing in the melody. The melodic intervals are small. Each phrase of the text is set in a phrase of music, and the phrases are of unequal length.

LINE SCORES—Bach: chorale in *Cantata No. 4, "Christ Lag in Todesbanden."*

F. MADRIGAL. A madrigal is a musical setting of a brief secular text, usually for a mixed vocal ensemble. The structures are usually sectional, contrapuntal imitation alternating with chordal writing. Madrigals are usually performed without instrumental support, though occasionally instruments are used to double the choral parts.

G. MOTET. A motet is a polyphonic, choral setting of a religious text (usually Latin). The typical motet structure resembles that of the madrigal. Some works called motets are composite forms. Although motets are usually performed without instrumental support, instruments occasionally are used to double the choral parts.

H. ANTHEM. An anthem is a choral setting of a religious text in English which is performed with instrumental (usually organ) accompaniment. Anthems for festival occasions sometimes require additional instruments (often brasses). A *verse anthem* is an anthem containing sections for solo voice. One which contains no such solos is called a *full anthem*.

II. **Composite forms.** Composite vocal forms are large works which may contain two or more *numbers* or movements.

A. SONG CYCLE. A song cycle is a group of several songs related in text and style.

B. CANTATA. A cantata is a setting of a dramatic or lyric text. Most cantatas have religious texts and are intended to be performed in church. A *choral cantata* may contain recitatives, arias, ensembles, choruses, and incidental instrumental music. A *solo cantata* usually contains no ensembles or choruses. A *chorale cantata* is based on a theme and text of a chorale.

LINE SCORES—Bach: *Cantata No. 4, "Christ Lag in Todesbanden."*

C. OPERA. An opera is a setting of a *libretto* (theatrical text) involving vocal and instrumental music, acting, costuming, and scenery. The productions vary in size. Some grandiose spectacles call for elaborately costumed vocal soloists, vocal ensembles, choral groups, and dancers; an augmented orchestra in the pit plus additional instrumentalists backstage; tons of scenic and lighting equipment; and complex stage machinery. Some modest productions require only two or three vocal soloists, piano accompaniment, one stage set, and a handful of properties.

The musical structure of operas also varies from simple to complex. In a *number opera* the structure may include recitatives, arias, ensembles, choruses, ballets, overtures (or preludes), and other incidental music. In the *continuous opera* the music is not set in separate numbers, and each act unfolds as an uninterrupted musico-dramatic unit. In both the continuous and the number opera there occurs a noticeable slowing of the action. The characters sing, rather than speak, their lines (many operas, however, contain some spoken dialogue), and much of the text is subjected to repetition and devoted to reflective commentary about events or situations in the plot.

LINE SCORES—Mozart: *The Marriage of Figaro;* Verdi: *Aïda.*

D. OPERETTA. An operetta is a diminutive opera, usually in a lighter vein and involving considerable spoken dialogue. Choruses, arias, and ensembles usually are less sophisticated in style than are those of opera.

E. ORATORIO. An oratorio is a setting of a text of religious or contemplative nature for vocal soloists, ensembles, and chorus with accompaniment (usually orchestral). The oratorio, intended for performance in a concert hall, involves no stagecraft. The usual structure resembles that of an opera, and there often is a narrator.

LINE SCORES—Handel: *Messiah.*

F. PASSION. A Passion, intended for performance in church, is an oratorio-like setting of one of the Gospel texts of the Passion of Christ.

G. MASS. The Mass (musically) is a setting of five portions of the Latin text of the solemn service of the Roman Catholic Church. These five sections, called the Ordinary of the Mass, include: *Kyrie eleison,* (Lord have mercy upon us), *Gloria in excelsis Deo* (Glory be to God on high), *Credo in unum Deum* (I believe in one God), *Sanctus—Benedictus* (Holy, holy, holy— Blessed is He who cometh in the name of the Lord), and *Agnus Dei* (Lamb of God). The Mass for the Dead (called the *Requiem* from the opening words "Requiem aeternam dona eis Domine," "Give them eternal rest, O Lord") includes the *Dies Irae* (Day of Wrath). The musical style of a *concert Mass* is such that its performance is more suited to the concert hall than to liturgical use in the church.

ANALYSES—Palestrina: *Pope Marcellus Mass.*

H. SERVICE. The Service is the Anglican (Episcopalian) equivalent of the Roman Catholic Mass, a setting of the Holy Communion Service from *The Book of Common Prayer.*

part 6

Musical Styles

A style is a characteristic manner of expression achieved by consistency in selection and manipulation of musical materials. Certain stylistic similarities are apparent among the individual works of any one composer, among compositions written at about the same time, among those intended to be performed in similar acoustical circumstances, and among works of composers of the same nationality. A consideration of musical styles may be facilitated by a somewhat arbitrary division of the history of music into periods within which, except for works reminiscent of an earlier age or prophetic of a later one, most of the music exhibits certain striking stylistic similarities.

Though most of the music heard today dates after the beginning of the Renaissance, some of the important developments in music before the Renaissance must be mentioned here.

The evolution of the art from its beginnings through the early years of Christianity can be traced only inadequately by such means as pictures of instruments, a few museum specimens of primitive instruments, references to music

59

in the Bible and other ancient writings including those of Plato and Aristotle, and a few fragments of written music, many of which have not been deciphered.

In the sixth century, Pope Gregory the Great collected and codified the Church's music which had developed from ancient Hebrew, Greek, Armenian, Syrian, and Byzantine music. The vast quantities of plainsong codified by Gregory and thus called Gregorian chant* constitute the most important examples of music surviving from the first thousand years of Christian era. Secular music was a healthy and flourishing branch of the art, but it was not disseminated and preserved by the church as was religious music.

From the tenth through the thirteenth centuries, wandering students called Goliards performed their monophonic songs throughout Europe. In the twelfth and thirteenth centuries, poet-musicians called troubadours, trouvères, and minnesinger wrote and performed love songs, songs for dancing, nonliturgical religious music, and other monophonic works. Among the names associated with this activity are those of Bernard de Ventadour (twelfth century), King Richard the Lion Hearted (1157–1199), Neidhart von Reuenthal (thirteenth century), Wolfram von Eschenbach (c. 1170–c. 1220), Walther von der Vogelweide (c. 1170–c. 1230), and Adam de la Halle (c. 1230–1287). The meistersinger continued activity in monophonic composition in Germany into the seventeenth century.

About a thousand years ago there developed an early polyphony called *organum*, in which a second vocal part was added to the plainsong melody. During this early polyphonic period, which terminated in the middle of the thirteenth century, many composers and theorists including Guido of Arezzo (c. 995–1050), Leonin (c. 1150–1185), and Perotin (c. 1160–1220) made such contributions as the invention of the staff, the use of the "do-re-mi" syllables for singing, and a system of notation to coordinate two or more parts having different rhythms.

---

* The asterisk is used throughout to refer to works given in the sections entitled "Abbreviated Analyses" and "Line Scores for Listening."

About the beginning of the fourteenth century there occurred a style change so marked that some progressive composers called their fourteenth century style *ars nova* (new art) and that of their immediate predecessors *ars antiqua* (old art). In the works of Philippe de Vitry (1290–1361), Guillaume de Machaut (c. 1300–1377), Francesco Landini (1325–1397), and others, more parts were added to musical textures, rhythm gained an extraordinary complexity, imitative counterpoint took on added importance, and the old harmony based on fourths and fifths began to be supplanted by tertian harmony.

In the music of John Dunstable (c. 1370–1453) a new emphasis upon tertian harmony results in a predominance of complete triads. The Burgundian composer Guillaume Dufay (c. 1400–1474) added to the old texture of voices of equal range and function a new, low voice which functioned as the bass. The Renaissance in music was ushered in with Jan van Ockeghem (c. 1430–1495), Jacob Obrecht (c. 1430–1505), and Josquin des Prez (c. 1450–1521), who were responsible for perfecting the use of imitative counterpoint for four or more equally important voices.

13

The Renaissance

The musical style of the Renaissance evolved during the fifteenth century and was disseminated by the church throughout most of Europe. Many of the Renaissance works performed today were composed for use in the church, though some were intended for performance in the home. Public concerts were unknown. Late in the sixteenth century the transition to a new style was evidenced by the growing importance of solo songs with accompaniment, instrumental music, works for keyboard instruments, Lutheran chorales, and the emphasis upon harmony which was inherent in these developments.

I. **Characteristics of style.** The style of church music, influenced by the acoustics of the cathedral and church, is marked by clarity, balance, and subtle contrasts. The secular music of the period bears a close stylistic resemblance to the sacred music.

  A. PERFORMANCE MEDIA. Instruments, used in secular music primarily to accompany dancing, sometimes support the voices in sacred music by duplicating the vocal lines. Although many performances today use transcriptions for modern instruments, authentic performances of Renaissance music employ instruments now obsolete. Works of the period were performed on such instruments as the *lute*, an instrument similar to the mandolin; the *harpsichord, clavichord,* and *virginal,* early keyboard instruments; the *recorder,* a soft-toned, wooden relative of the flute; the *shawm,* an early double-reed instrument; the *cornett,* a wooden instrument whose soft tones were produced in the same way as the tones of brass instruments; and *viols,* a string family which later was replaced by modern bowed instruments. The principal instrument in church music then, as now, was the pipe organ.

  B. RHYTHM. Most of the music is propelled by a steady pulse lacking heavy accents. Contrasts of tempo sometimes occur within a work but contrasts of meter are more important, sections in triple meter relieving the usual duple. Textual overlapping in choral polyphony creates a rich interplay of accents between the voice parts. Each part possesses a remarkably independent rhythmic life with accents created by higher pitch and longer duration placed in accordance with the accents of the text. In sections in which all voices sing the same syllables at the same time (called *chordal style*) this polyrhythmic vitality is absent.

C. MELODY. The melodies, submerged in counterpoint, are not as prominent as are melodies in later styles. Many entire religious compositions are based on a "borrowed" melody such as a Gregorian chant or a secular song used as a *cantus firmus* (fixed melody) and sung in notes of long duration, usually by the tenor. The melodic movement is preponderantly step-wise with a few narrow leaps. The modal scales are used.

D. TEXTURE. The characteristic texture is polyphonic, with four or more equally prominent voices, although in late sixteenth century music the soprano gains in importance. The voices may begin one at a time in imitation or begin all at once in chordal style. A combination of these techniques may also be used. The choir may be divided into two groups which are "opposed" to each other in *antiphonal* (sound-against-sound) contrasts, a procedure especially important in the music of the Venetian composers. Contrapuntal imitation is used extensively, especially free imitation of the first few notes of each subject. Many compositions contain two or more voices in canon while the remaining voices imitate freely. The characteristic chord, the triad, originates as a by-product of contrapuntal activity. Sections of chordal style, in which the contrapuntal interest is minimized and the harmonic element emphasized, are distinguished from later harmonic writing by the frequent occurrence of triads from which the middle note is omitted and by a certain aimlessness (for modern ears) resulting from the absence of normal chord progressions toward a tonal center. There is considerable dissonance, but the clashes are so controlled that they contribute to rhythmic momentum and to melodic smoothness more than to tension.

E. STRUCTURE AND FORMS. The most important forms are the Mass, motet, madrigal, Passion, fantasia, and *toccata* ("touch-piece" for keyboard instrument). Phrases are irregular in length. Internal cadences are gentle and are often concealed by the completion of one phrase in one voice being overlapped by the beginning of the next phrase in another voice. The typical work consists of several subjects, usually one subject per phrase of text, each of which is stated and imitated in successive expositions.

II. Representative composers

A. JOSQUIN DES PREZ (Flemish, but lived in Italy; c. 1450–1521). Renaissance style became firmly established in the music of Josquin. His works include the *Missa pange lingua* and other Masses, motets such as *Ave Maria*, and secular music. Intricate canons permeate the texture of his early compositions. In his later works the technical complexities of imitative counterpoint are infused with a lyric warmth, yielding a reserved and expressive style. Most of his choral compositions employ four voices.

B. GIOVANNI PIERLUIGI DA PALESTRINA (Italian; 1525–1594). Most of Palestrina's compositions were written for use in the Roman Catholic Church. His Masses and motets tend more toward beauty and purity of sound than toward dramaticism. He also composed madrigals in a style closely resembling that of his church music. The course of each contrapuntal voice undulates unhurriedly and smoothly within a narrow and fairly high range. The texture is light and transparent. The overlapping of the end of one phrase by the beginning of the next results in a steady, seamless flow of sound. Among his well known works are the *Missa Papae Marcelli (Pope Marcellus Mass)** and the motet, *Adoremus te Christe.*

C. ORLANDUS LASSUS (Flemish, but lived in Italy; c. 1532–1594). The Masses, motets, and madrigals of Lassus (also called Orlando di Lasso) number more than twelve hundred. In works such as the *Penetential Psalms,* the motet, *Tristis est anima mea,* and the madrigal, *O che bon echo,* the imitative counterpoint common to Renaissance style is suffused with fervor, dramatic changes of mood, and strong and interesting rhythms uncommon in Renaissance style. Among his works are settings of German, French, and Italian, as well as Latin texts.

D. WILLIAM BYRD (English; 1543–1623). Although he wrote madrigals, secular songs, pieces for string ensemble, and keyboard works, most of Byrd's music is religious. He composed Services and anthems for the Anglican Church and Masses (including the *Masses for Four and Five Voices*) and motets (including *Ego sum panis vivus*) for the Roman Catholic Church. There is more dissonance in his music than in that of most of his contemporaries, and text-painting is quite important. The texture is prevailingly contrapuntal with frequent contrasting sections of chordal writing.

E. GIOVANNI GABRIELI (Italian; 1557–1612). Much of Gabrieli's music exhibits the marked contrasts characteristic of Venetian style. His *Sonata pian e forte* opposes the sound of a choir composed of a cornett and three trombones against the sound of a second choir composed of a violin and three trombones. This work, an extremely early example of music in which contrasts of loud and soft are featured, stands as a beginning of the history of the concerto. Among Gabrieli's other compositions are his *Canzonas for Brass Choirs* and a number of madrigals and motets, many of which have instrumental accompaniments.

III. Additional listening suggestions

A. MADRIGALS AND OTHER SECULAR VOCAL MUSIC

1. Clement Jannequin (French; c. 1485–1560): *Le Chant des Oiseaux*
2. Luca Marenzio (Italian; 1533–1599): *S'io parto, i'moro*
3. Thomas Morley (English; 1557–1603): *Now Is the Month of Maying*
4. Don Carlo Gesualdo (Italian; c. 1560–1613): *Dolcissima mia vita*
5. John Dowland (English; 1563–1626): Songs from the *Second Book of Ayres*
6. Hans Leo Hassler (German; 1564–1612): *Tanzen und Springen*
7. John Wilbye (English; c. 1574–1638): *Flora Gave Me Fairest Flowers*
8. Thomas Weelkes (English; c. 1575–1623): *O Care, Thou Wilt Dispatch Me*
9. Orlando Gibbons (English; 1583–1625): *The Silver Swan*

B. MOTETS, MASSES, AND OTHER SACRED VOCAL MUSIC

    1. Cristóbal de Morales (Spanish; c. 1500–1553): *Lamentabatur Jacob*
    2. Thomas Tallis (English; c. 1505–1585): *Lamentations of Jeremiah*
    3. Tomás Luis de Victoria (Spanish; c. 1548–1611): *Ave Maria*

C. INSTRUMENTAL MUSIC

    1. Luis Milán (Spanish; c. 1500–c. 1561): *Three Pavanes*
    2. Andrea Gabrieli (Italian; c. 1520–1586): *Canzona francese, deta Pour ung plaisir*

14

The Baroque

The Baroque period began late in the sixteenth century with a new style which was called *stile moderno*. A multitude of new forms, instruments, methods, and ideals resulted from the ensuing stylistic revolution. Of course, some composers remained loyal to Renaissance style, *stile antico*. By the early eighteenth century the styles of the late or "high" Baroque had crystallized. Sacred and secular music were of about equal importance. The new opera was performed for the public while concerts as well as opera were given in the courts of royalty.

I. **Characteristics of style.** As in most revolutionary periods, the diverse styles of the early Baroque generally hold in common those elements which negate the principles of the old order. Sixteenth-century polyphony gave way to homophonic writing (counterpoint returned to favor soon, however); the major and minor scales gradually replaced the archaic modes; chords, which had occurred in the Renaissance as by-products of contrapuntal activity, became in the Baroque deliberately constructed entities, and instrumental music assumed a new importance. The carefully detailed massive grandeur of the late Baroque springs stylistically from Venetian antiphonal choir style, Italian lyricism, French ornamentation and dance rhythms, and German formality, solidity, and directness.

A. PERFORMANCE MEDIA. In the Baroque period instrumental music gained in importance as dance music became stylized as music for listening rather than exclusively for dancing. In choral works, instead of duplicating the choral lines, the instruments often accompany the voices in independent lines. The orchestra is not standardized, but often includes flutes, oboes, bassoons, and keyboard instruments plus strings. A keyboard instrument, often a harpsichord, is involved in most performances of Baroque music. Authentic performances today also employ such obsolete instruments as *viola da gamba*, *viola d'amore*, and the brilliant "Bach" trumpets whose pitch is several degrees higher than that of the standard modern trumpet.

B. RHYTHM. Two diametrically opposed rhythmic practices prevail. In vocal recitatives, the rhythm is free, dictated by that of the text. Elsewhere a strong and relentless beat is accentuated by changing harmonies and by repeated notes in the accompaniment. Many works are based on one rhythmic pattern and employ one unchanging tempo.

C. MELODY. Baroque melodies, more conspicuous than those of involved Renaissance polyphony, are flowing, sometimes highly ornamented melodies spun out over chordal accompaniment. There are frequent striking *melismas* (several notes sung on the same syllable). Emotion-charged words such as "death," "cross," "sorrow," and so forth, are frequently text-painted by disjunct or chromatic contours and by dissonance in the accompaniment. Melodic subjects are usually continuous melodies evolved by repetitions and modifications of a motive.

D. TEXTURE. Early Baroque works are usually uncompromisingly homophonic, but in the late Baroque music a full and sonorous harmony is created by contrapuntal lines passing through chords. One important common practice is the use of the *basso continuo* or *figured bass*. These terms refer to the appearance in the score of a continuous written-out bass part with figures (numbers) representing the chords which are to be played. In a manner quite like that of the modern dance-band piano player, the Baroque keyboard performer, who often was the composer, played the written bass part and improvised the harmony from the figures while the bass instrument or instruments reinforced the bottom part. The instruments involved in performing the figured bass are often referred to as the *continuo*.

E. STRUCTURE AND FORMS. The Baroque ideal of sustaining one mood throughout a work is apparent in the many compositions based on one subject. Such Renaissance forms as Passion, fantasia, and toccata are further developed in the Baroque period. The new forms—opera, oratorio, cantata, chorale prelude, trio sonata, concerto grosso, and overture—all stemmed from earlier forms. Baroque works called "sonata" or "concerto" are not sonatas or concerti in the modern sense of the words, the sonata-allegro form being non-existent in Baroque music. A Baroque sonata might be a work in several dance-like movements for unaccompanied instrument or for one or two instruments plus continuo. In the many binary forms the second part is usually complementary to the first. Among the important Baroque formal innovations were the *aria da capo*, a work of two sections in which the *da capo* ("to the head") effects a repetition of the first section after the second; the "Italian overture," a prefatory work in three sections, fast-slow-fast; the "French overture," a prefatory work in two sections, the first slow with important dotted note rhythms and the second fast in fugal style.

II. Representative composers

A. CLAUDIO MONTEVERDI (Italian; 1567–1643). The transition from the style of the late Renaissance to that of the early Baroque can be traced in the compositions of Monteverdi. His early madrigals feature imitative counterpoint while many of the later ones are scored for solo voice with continuo. His Masses and other church music are imbued with Baroque dramaticism, although the texture is essentially one of sixteenth-century polyphony.

The operas of Monteverdi exhibit most of the components of today's opera, although they were written during the infancy of the musical drama. Monteverdi's instrumental forces for *Orfeo,* which employed strings, harpsichords, lutes, portable pipe organs, cornetts, recorders, trombones, and trumpets, comprised one of the earliest ensembles which might be called an orchestra. The passages scored for these instruments include the first opera overture and other instrumental sections which use instrumental effects such as the tremolo for projecting dramatic situation and action. Monteverdi's compositions include *Il Combattimento di Tancredi e Clorinda, L'Incoronazione de Poppea,* and *Lagrime d'Amante.*

B. JEAN BAPTISTE LULLY (Italian, but lived in France; 1632–1687). Virtually the founder of French opera (with *Cadmus et Hermione*), Lully originated the French overture. In his numerous ballets he introduced new dance types, including the minuet and bourrée. One of his important innovations as an orchestral leader (conductors were then unknown) was demanding of his players more meticulous performances than had been customary. Lully also wrote a number of sacred works, including the *Miserere.*

C. ARCANGELO CORELLI (Italian; 1653–1713). Among the early important concerti grossi are those of Corelli. His concerti, which are usually in five or more short movements, are performed by the full group of strings and continuo contrasted with the concertino of two violins, cello, and harpsichord. In his *sonatas da chiesa,* the number of movements is standardized at four. His recorded works include the *Christmas Concerto, Op. 6, No. 8,* and *La Folia.*

D. HENRY PURCELL (English; c. 1659–1695). The style of Purcell stands out from that of his contemporaries by virtue of its high degree of expressiveness and originality of harmony and its sensitive handling of sharp dissonance. Among his works are an opera, *Dido and Aeneas;** religious compositions including anthems and Services; trio sonatas; other chamber music including the *Fantasias for Viols da Gamba;* and pieces for keyboard instrument including the *Voluntary in D Major.*

E. ALESSANDRO SCARLATTI (Italian; c. 1660–1725). Known as the founder of Neapolitan opera, the dominant type of opera for nearly a century, Scarlatti was among those instrumental in establishing the da capo aria and the "Italian overture." Scarlatti is also credited with increasing the importance of the strings while decreasing the importance of the harpsichord in the opera orchestra. Among his compositions are the opera, *Il Trionfo dell'Onore,* chamber music such as the *Sonata a Quattro in D Minor,* and church music including a *Stabat Mater.*

F. ANTONIO VIVALDI (Italian; c. 1675–1741). Vivaldi's compositions include many vocal pieces, but most of his works performed today are selected from the hundreds of solo violin concerti and concerti grossi for which he established the three-movement (fast-slow-fast) form. Among them are *L'Estro Armonico* and *The Four Seasons.* In the elaborate virtuoso passages which call for fast arpeggios and wide melodic leaps, his concerti evidence some important expansions in violin technique.

G. JOHANN SEBASTIAN BACH (German; 1685–1750). A catalogue of Bach's works includes examples of virtually all Baroque forms and types except opera. Many of his compositions, such as *"Christ Lag in Todesbanden"** and other cantatas, the "Christmas" and "Easter" oratorios, the *Magnificat in D*, the *Mass in B Minor*, the *Passion according to St. Matthew*, and the chorale preludes, were written for use in the church. Others, including the *Brandenburg Concerti*, the *English* and *French Suites* for harpsichord, the *Goldberg Variations* for harpsichord, and the four orchestral suites, were conceived as entertainment for a courtly audience. Works such as the two- and three-part inventions were written as instruction pieces for students. Bach's harmony is solid and rich and has a relatively high degree of dissonance. The counterpoint is harmonically controlled and there is a bit more chromaticism in his lines than in those of his contemporaries. Many of his compositions are based on melodies borrowed from his own earlier works or from the works of others, a common practice of the time. Many of his religious compositions are based on Lutheran chorales. His contrapuntal works, particularly the organ fugues and those in *The Art of the Fugue*, are remarkable for the intensive use of all devices of imitation.

H. DOMENICO SCARLATTI (Italian; 1685–1757). In Domenico Scarlatti's several hundred pieces for harpsichord are found many passages requiring new techniques which he contributed to the art of keyboard playing. Quick arpeggios, wide leaps, rapidly repeated notes, and crossing of hands, all were foreign to the organ style which dominated Baroque keyboard music. He wrote operas, Masses, cantatas, and other works, but his keyboard fugues (among them the familiar *"Cat's Fugue"*) and sonatas are the works for which he is most celebrated. His sonatas are mostly binary works, based on one theme, in which the transitions between sections sometimes hint at the idea of thematic development.

I. GEORGE FREDERICK HANDEL (German, but lived in England; 1685–1759). The works of Handel, most of which were written for English audiences, often assume monumental proportions. There are strong influences of Italian melodic writing and of the Venetian antiphonal style. The harmony is simpler and the style less chromatic than that of Bach. Handelian rhythm is characteristically vigorous and compelling. Among his important works are oratorios such as *Messiah,** *Judas Maccabaeus*, and *Israel in Egypt*; operas, including *Julius Caesar* and *Xerxes* (which contains the aria, "Ombra mai fu," known in transcription as the "Largo"); the *Chandos Anthems* and other vocal music; harpsichord music such as *The Harmonious Blacksmith*; and orchestral music such as the *Concerti Grossi, Op. 6*, the *Royal Fireworks Music*, and the *Water Music*.

III. Additional listening suggestions

A. OPERAS

1. Jacopo Peri (Italian; 1561–1633): *Euridice*
2. John Blow (English; 1649–1708): *Venus and Adonis*
3. Jean-Philippe Rameau (French; 1683–1764): *Hippolyte et Aricie, Les Indes Galantes*
4. John Gay (English; 1685–1732) and
   John Christopher Pepusch (German, but lived in England; 1667–1752): *The Beggar's Opera*
5. Giovanni Battista Pergolesi (Italian; 1710–1736): *La Serva Padrona*

B. ORATORIOS, PASSIONS, AND OTHER VOCAL MUSIC

1. Giulio Caccini (Italian; c. 1558–c. 1615): "Amarilli mia bella" from a collection, *Le Nuove Musiche*
2. Heinrich Schütz (German; 1585–1672): *The Christmas Story; Requiem (Musicalische Exequien)*
3. Giacomo Carissimi (Italian; 1605–1674): *Jepthe*
4. Orazio Benevoli (Italian; 1605–1672): *Festival Mass for Fifty-three Voices*
5. Marc-Antoine Charpentier (French; c. 1634–1704): *Magnificat*
6. Michel Delalande (French; 1657–1726): *De Profundis*

C. KEYBOARD WORKS

1. Jan Pieterszoon Sweelinck (Dutch; 1562–1621): *Fantasia in Echo Style*
2. Girolamo Frescobaldi (Italian; 1583–1643): *Fiori Musicali*
3. Samuel Scheidt (German; 1587–1654): *Tablatura Nova*
4. Dietrich Buxtehude (Danish, but lived in Germany; 1637–1707): *Prelude, Fugue, and Chaconne*
5. Johann Kuhnau (German; 1660–1722): *Biblical Sonatas*
6. Georg Böhm (German; 1661–1733): *Chorale Partita*
7. François Couperin (French; 1668–1733): *Pièces de Clavecin*

D. ORCHESTRAL MUSIC

1. Giuseppe Torelli (Italian; c. 1650–1708): *Christmas Concerto, Op. 8*
2. Georg Philipp Telemann (German; 1681–1767): *Concerto in G for Viola and Strings*
3. Pietro Locatelli (Italian; 1695–1764): *Concerti Grossi, Op. 1*
4. Carl Philipp Emanuel Bach (German; 1714–1788): *Symphonies Nos. 1 and 3*
5. Johann Christian Bach (German; 1735–1782): *Sinfonia Concertante*

15

The Classic Period

Throughout the history of composed music run two aesthetic codes, classicism and romanticism, one sometimes figuring more prominently than the other at a given time. In classicism, which favors stability, clarity, symmetry, and conformity to tradition and established practices, content must be adapted to the restraints of form, the manner of expression being as important as the thought to be expressed. Classic art is expressive, but in the objective manner of a more or less disinterested observer rather than in the subjective manner of one who is personally involved. The romantic aesthetic is less concerned with tradition than with artistic self-expression. If an established form cannot contain a particular thought, the form is expanded or discarded. In contrast to the objectivity of classicism, romantic art emphasizes individuality, subjective expression, and nonconformity.

Several times during the history of music there have been periods during which classic thought prevailed. The capitalized term "Classic," however, is usually applied to the period beginning about 1750 and extending into the early nineteenth century.

Late in the Baroque period some composers (including Telemann, Couperin, Domenico Scarlatti, and C. P. E. Bach) abandoned the vigorous and impressive Baroque style, preferring instead a pretty, pleasant, frivolous style with simple harmonies and rhythms, a minimum of counterpoint, and florid, highly embellished melodies. This style, called Rococo, was suited to the performance skills of the many amateurs among the nobility.

Elements of Rococo style were combined with new and significant practices by a school of Viennese composers who created an international style sometimes called "Viennese Classic," which combined French, German, and Italian regional temperaments. Other important compositional activity during the period centered at the court of Mannheim and in Milan.

I. **Characteristics of style.** The performance media and the forms which replaced those of Baroque music are still in common use.

   A. PERFORMANCE MEDIA. A light, transparent sound results from voices and instruments sounding in their medium-high registers, avoiding the density of the low and the brilliance of the high registers. In the Classic period instrumental music is more important than vocal music. The piano is the favorite keyboard instrument; the violin is firmly established as the principal orchestral and chamber music instrument; and the string quartet is the standard instrumental chamber ensemble. The instrumentation of the orchestra is fairly well standardized. The typical Classic orchestra has as a nucleus a string choir of fewer than thirty players. The woodwinds, numbering two each of flutes, oboes, and bassoons, are given frequent melodic passages while a pair of horns, to which trumpets are sometimes added, sustain the harmonies, perform fanfare patterns, and occasionally assist melodically. The timpani provide a rhythmic accentuation, often in league with the brasses. The opera orchestra and that used for some late symphonies is larger, adding a piccolo, a pair of clarinets, a trio of trombones, and additional percussion instruments. The strings are used almost continuously, and the double basses seldom operate independently of the cellos.

B. RHYTHM. The rhythm is simple and regular, with infrequent changes of pace within a movement. The propulsion stems from rhythmic patterns in the accompaniment or from the bass accenting the beats while other voices play the off-beats.

C. MELODY. Thematic melodies are usually short tunes similar in character to those associated with singing, dancing, marching, and hunting. An important type of melody is the "singing allegro," a sustained line in long notes flowing over a rhythmic accompaniment. Transitions between themes are often rapid "passage work," sequences of scales and arpeggios.

D. TEXTURE. The melody usually sounds in the highest voice although, in string quartets, the instruments often take turns at providing melody and accompaniment. Much of the keyboard music has but two real parts, one for each hand, the right hand playing the melody while the left supplies the bass and harmony. In most of the music counterpoint is relatively unimportant, though in some of the later works imitative counterpoint is a feature in the development sections. The harmony is not as rich as that of the late Baroque, and there is less tension. The contrast of keys is a basic feature of the style, one key being established at the beginning of a piece, others explored in the middle, and the original key reintroduced at the end.

E. STRUCTURE AND FORMS. Important large forms of Classic music include overture, theme and variations, sonata-allegro, sonatina, sonata, concerto, symphony, string trio, quartet, quintet, divertimento, opera, oratorio, and Mass. Themes are treated in a craftsman-like fashion, making the most music from the fewest ideas. The proportions of the forms are usually clearly defined by the musical punctuation. Phrases are generally short, clear, and regular. Cadences are frequent, strongly establishing tonality. Binary forms occur infrequently (although sonata-allegro developed from binary structures). Ternary and rondo forms are common.

II. Representative composers

A. CRISTOPH WILLIBALD VON GLUCK (German; 1714–1787). Gluck's early operas display the prevailing Italian style in which dramatic truth is less important than pyrotechnic display arias for the soloists. These conditions are remedied in his "reform" operas, including *Alceste* and *Orfeo ed Euridice*, which are noteworthy for simplicity, rational plots, subordination of the music to the libretto, and expressive melodies.

B. FRANZ JOSEPH HAYDN (Austrian; 1732–1809). The refinement and clarification of some of the forms developed by his predecessors are evident in the works of Haydn. The early quartets and symphonies trace his steps toward crystallizing those forms and toward solving the problem of distributing the harmony, which had been provided by the continuo, among the various instruments. His themes are lively and good-humored, with the sturdy directness of peasant dance tunes. The phrases are usually regular, with strong cadences. Many of his sonata-allegro movements depend more upon contrast of key than of theme, and symphonic first movements usually begin with a slow introduction. Third movements are minuets. Among Haydn's works frequently performed today are the *Cello Concerto in D, Op. 101*; two oratorios, *The Creation* and *The Seasons*; the *Missa Solemnis in D Minor* and other Masses; *Quartets, Op. 76*; *The Seven Last Words of Christ*; and *Symphonies Nos. 45, 88, 92, 94,* 96, 99, 100, 101, 102, 103, and 104*.

C. WOLFGANG AMADEUS MOZART (Austrian; 1756–1791). Mozart's music is slightly more sophisticated than that of Haydn, with a buoyant gaiety which sometimes tends to conceal some of its more profound aspects. Melodic chromaticism is more pronounced, and the phrases are frequently irregular in length. The themes often contrast sharply, one chromatic and the other diatonic. There is some fugal writing, especially in development sections and in choral works. His later compositions tend toward "storm and stress" dramaticism, prophetic of the approach of the Romantic period. Some of Mozart's operas, *The Marriage of Figaro,* *Don Giovanni,* and *The Magic Flute,* are among the earliest operas still regularly produced. Included among his well-known works are the concerti for piano K. 466, K. 482, K. 488, K. 491, K. 537 and K. 595; concerti for violin K. 218, and K. 219; *Eine Kleine Nachtmusik,* *K. 525*; quartets K. 387, K. 421, K. 428, K. 458, K. 464, K. 465, K. 499, K. 575, K. 589, and K. 590; the *Requiem, K. 626*; piano sonatas K. 282, K. 283, K. 284, K. 331, K. 457, K. 545, K. 570, and K. 576; symphonies K. 201, K. 297, K. 385, K. 425, K. 504, K. 543, K. 550, and K. 551; the *Mass in C Minor, K. 427*; and many other compositions. (The symbol *K.* or *K.V.* appended to a title refers to *Köchel's Verzeichniss* [index] which lists in chronological order more than six hundred of Mozart's works.)

D. LUDWIG VAN BEETHOVEN (German; 1770–1827). Beethoven's earliest works resemble those of Haydn and Mozart, and all of his compositions adhere (although not strictly) to Classic forms. His *Symphony No. 3* and later works, however, are imbued with romanticism, abounding in gruff good humor, impulsiveness, programmatic connotations, tremendous climaxes after long suspense, and "storm and stress" dramaticism. Beethoven's orchestra is nearly double the size of that used by Haydn and assigns more important parts to the wind instruments. Beethoven's piano writing often uses dark, thick chords in the lower octaves, and his choral writing gives to voices melodies of an instrumental nature. His themes are usually warm and song-like or short, pregnant ideas in which repeated-note rhythms are important. While the works of many of his contemporaries often sound somewhat alike, each of Beethoven's compositions is unique. His innovations include varying the number of movements in the sonata form; introducing vocal solos and choruses in a symphony; varying the number of themes and introducing new material in the development section and in the coda of sonata-allegro movements; using a *scherzo* (literally a "joke") rather than the traditional minuet for symphonic third movements; reversing the tempo relationships of the two middle movements; reintroducing themes from earlier movements; and passing from one movement to another without pause. Among Beethoven's works frequently performed are the five piano concerti; the *Concerto in D for Violin, Op. 61;* the *Missa Solemnis in D, Op. 123;* quartets Op. 18, Op. 59, Op. 74, Op. 95, Op. 127, Op. 130, and Op. 133; the five sonatas for cello and thirty-two piano sonatas; violin sonatas Op. 23, Op. 24, and Op. 47; the nine symphonies; four piano trios; and the *Variations in C Minor* for piano.

III. Additional listening suggestions

A. SONATAS

  1. Giuseppe Tartini (Italian; 1692–1770): *Violin Sonata in G Minor*
  2. Muzio Clementi (Italian; 1752–1832): *Sonatinas, Op. 36*
  3. Friedrich Kuhlau (German; 1786–1832): *Sonatinas, Op. 20, Op. 55*

B. CONCERTI

  1. Michael Haydn (Austrian; 1737–1806): *Concerto for Viola, Keyboard, and Orchestra*
  2. Giovanni Paisiello (Italian; 1740–1816): *Concerto in C Major for Piano*
  3. Luigi Boccherini (Italian; 1743–1805): *Concerto in B-flat for Cello*
  4. Francesco Rosetti (Italian; 1750–1792): *Concerto in E-flat for Horn*
  5. Jean Baptiste Viotti (Italian; 1753–1824): *Concerto No. 4 in D for Violin*

C. SYMPHONIES

  1. Giovanni Battista Sammartini (Italian; 1701–1775): *Symphony in G*
  2. Karl Ditters von Dittersdorf (German; 1739–1799): *Symphony in E-flat*
  3. Gaetano Brunetti (Italian; c. 1740–1808): *Symphony No. 33 in C Minor*
  4. Étienne Méhul (French; 1763–1817): *Symphony No. 1 in G Minor*

D. CHAMBER MUSIC

1. Franz Xaver Richter (German; 1709–1789): *Quartet in C, Op. 5, No. 1*
2. Karl Stamitz (German; 1746–1801): *Quartet in A Major, Op. 14*
3. Johann Hummel (Hungarian; 1778–1837): *Quartet in G, Op. 30, No. 2*

E. MISCELLANEOUS

1. André Grétry (French; 1741–1813): *Céphale et Procris* (ballet suite taken from opera of same name)
2. Domenico Cimarosa (Italian; 1749–1801): *Il Matrimonio Segreto* (opera)
3. Ignaz Pleyel (German; 1757–1831): *Symphonie Concertante No. 5*

16

The

Romantic Period

Although romanticism has prevailed in several periods during the history of music, the capitalized term "Romantic" is usually applied to the most recent such period, which extended from about 1810 until about 1890. Two schools of thought are evident in Romantic music. One school, holding that music is an independent art capable of conveying in its own terms what is to be expressed, created works which are Romantic in timbre, rhythm, melody, and harmony, but which are molded in the traditional forms of absolute music. The second school of thought, holding that the effectiveness of music should be heightened by alliance with other arts, especially literature, created the many programmatic works of the period.

I. **Characteristics of style.** Nineteenth-century Romantic music, which still dominates concert and recital programs more than fifty years after the mainstream of the period terminated, is characterized by an emotional and dramatic style conceived for virtuoso performers and is subjectively expressive of a wide gamut of moods and emotions.

A. PERFORMANCE MEDIA. Most Romantic works are intended for performance in the concert hall, in the opera house, or in the intimacy of the salon; the music for the church declined in importance during the period. The performance media reflect this situation, the large symphony orchestra being the favorite concert medium while piano and solo voice with piano accompaniment are the favorite media for music for the salon. Most Romantic orchestral works require a large orchestra, with a larger string section than is necessary to perform Classic music and with additional instruments such as piccolo, clarinets, English horn, oboes, trombones, tuba, harp, and various percussion instruments. Instrumental timbre is used as a means of expressing moods and emotions, the art of orchestration being an almost independent facet of the art of composition.

B. RHYTHM. Rhythm, important in the portrayal of moods and emotions, is complicated and flexible. Slowing and quickening of the pulse, meter changes, syncopation, and complex patterns all contribute to rhythmic expressiveness. The music abounds in indications for *ritardando, accelerando, rubato*, sudden dramatic tempo changes, and unexpected pauses. With the terms establishing tempo often appear other terms suggestive of mood, such as *amoroso* (lovingly), *brilliante* (brilliantly), *con calore* (with warmth), *doloroso* (sadly), *grandioso* (with grandeur), *morendo* (dying), *con sentimento* (with feeling), and *teneramente* (tenderly).

C. MELODY. A Romantic melody is a highly personal and unique utterance. The use of pre-existent melodies, which had been quite common in earlier periods, is in Romantic music a practice condoned only in occasional programmatic quotations of folk songs or well-known tunes like the *Dies Irae* or *A Mighty Fortress Is Our God*, or in sets of variations on a theme whose source is acknowledged in the title. While compact tunes of the Classic period are often equally effective in any of several diverse settings, the more rambling melodies of Romantic music are often more effective when played in a particular harmonic situation by a specific instrument. Romantic melodies written for voices show the influence of instrumental melodic style, with disjunct contour and chromatic movement. Occasionally the modal scales are used for archaic effect.

D. TEXTURE. The rather heavy texture of most of this music features a prominent melody supported by chords. The harmony is rich, with considerable dissonance used to create a high degree of emotional tension. The prevailing homophonic texture is sometimes relieved by free imitative counterpoint as the melodies are passed about from voice to voice. The works of some composers late in the period exhibit a concentration upon harmonically-controlled counterpoint. The highly chromatic harmony employs, interchangeably, chords from major and minor keys. Modulation, which in older music had been a means of changing from one strongly established key to another, is sometimes used so insistently in late Romantic music that the tonality is blurred.

E. STRUCTURE AND FORMS. The typical forms are miniature or gigantic, the small forms being favored for intimate salon music and the large for concert performance. In addition to expanded versions of forms inherited from the Classic period, the important Romantic forms include the tone poem, character piece, concert overture, art song, and rhapsody. There are also hybrid forms such as the symphony-cantata and the program symphony. Phrases are usually irregular, and cadences are often concealed. Thematic transformation is important as a means of unifying cyclical works. The leitmotiv idea is used extensively in programmatic works.

II. Representative composers

A. CARL MARIA VON WEBER (German; 1786–1826). Weber is generally acknowledged to be the founder of German romantic opera. Breaking from the Italian operatic tradition, which had dominated the form since its inception, Weber based his operas on traditional Germanic stories, filling the music with folk-like songs and dances. His operas, of which only the brilliant and dramatic overtures are still heard with any regularity, included the landmark *Der Freischütz* (the first German romantic opera), *Euryanthe*, and *Oberon*.

B. GIOACCHINO ROSSINI (Italian; 1792–1868). Rossini's bright and facile style, with lilting Italian melodies, vivacious rhythm, and uncomplicated harmony, is well represented by his opera, *The Barber of Seville*, and by the overtures to his other stage works including *Semiramide*, *La Cenerentola*, *La Gazza Ladra*, *The Italian in Algiers*, and *William Tell*. His religious compositions, the style of which is also theatrical, include the familiar *Stabat Mater*.

C. FRANZ SCHUBERT (Austrian; 1797–1828). Schubert's instrumental works exhibit characteristic Romantic traits: tremendous climaxes, rich harmony, and extended, song-like melodies. Although some of his works are cyclic (and cyclical forms are usually associated with Romantic music), the forms adhere in other details to those of Classic music. In his lieder, rhythm, melody, and harmony all are used to reflect the words and to create mood, an accompanying motive often serving as the unifying force. Among Schubert's works are the *"Unfinished" Symphony;* the *C Major Symphony* called *"The Great";* the string quartet, *"Death and the Maiden";* the *"Trout" Quintet; Der Erlkönig,* Der Wanderer,* Serenade,* and some six hundred other lieder.

D. HECTOR BERLIOZ (French; 1803–1869). All of Berlioz' compositions bear programmatic titles, although the extramusical narration and description is presented within the framework of expanded Classic forms. His occasional use of orchestral timbre as a primary rather than secondary consideration was an important step toward establishing orchestration as an almost independent branch of the composer's craft. Berlioz' orchestra may include such instruments as harps, cornets, extra bassoons, and an extra tuba. His scores use such vivid effects as mixtures of high flute with low trombone, and solo clarinet with bass drum and timpani. The familiar *Symphonie Fantastique* employs a leitmotiv-like subject called an *idée fixe* (fixed idea) to represent the principal character. Among his other works are *Harold in Italy*, a symphony; a *Requiem;* operas, including *The Trojans;* oratorios such as *L'Enfance du Christ;* and songs.

E. FELIX MENDELSSOHN (German; 1809–1847). The music of Mendelssohn (who is sometimes called Mendelssohn-Bartholdy) is Classic in the careful restraint of content by form, in lucidity of texture, and in balanced structure, but his music is Romantic in its extended melodic lyricism, its use of several contrasting themes in each movement, its connection of movements without pause, and its warmth of feeling. In the works bearing programmatic titles, realistic description or narration is not attempted, the titles indicating only the source of inspiration. The concerti are conceived for virtuoso performers. His better known works include the *"Scotch," "Italian,"* and *"Reformation"* symphonies; incidental music for *A Midsummer Night's Dream;* the *Violin Concerto in E Minor;* Elijah,* and other oratorios; piano pieces; and chamber music.

F. FRÉDÉRIC CHOPIN (Polish, but lived in France; 1810–1849). Chopin composed almost exclusively for the piano. Many of his works, intended for performance in the intimacy of the salon, are in ternary form. The descriptive title is often the only programmatic element present. His themes are more often repeated than varied and developed. Many of his works, which include such well-known compositions as *Piano Concertos Nos. 1 and 2; Etudes, Op. 10** and *Op. 25;* mazurkas, nocturnes, polonaises; *Preludes, Op. 28;* and *Sonatas Nos. 2 and 3,* are imbued with the spirit of Polish nationalism.

G. ROBERT SCHUMANN (German; 1810–1856). Schumann's compositions for the virtuoso pianist include the well-known *Piano Concerto in A Minor,** *Symphonic Etudes, Carnaval,* and the *C Major Fantasia.* His other works remaining in the repertory include four symphonies, a cello concerto, chamber music, song cycles such as *Frauenlieben und Leben,* and many lieder. Many of his piano works are sets of short pieces unified cyclically by the transformation of a germinal motive. The music is not essentially programmatic, although many works bear extramusical titles. Textures are heavy, and sections of lyric smoothness and impetuous dramaticism are often juxtaposed. The piano accompaniments in Schumann's lieder, many of which are concluded by pianistic codas, attain a special importance and are often as important as the vocal line.

H. FRANZ LISZT (Hungarian; 1811–1886). Classic forms are not common in the works of Liszt. Even those entitled "concerto" or "sonata" are, like the *Faust Symphony,* usually free forms influenced by a program. His piano works, which include *Funérailles,* the *Sonata in B Minor,* and the *Hungarian Rhapsodies,* are virtuoso display pieces of the highest order of technical difficulty. His piano concerti are part of the standard repertory. Liszt is generally acknowledged to be the originator of the tone poem, of which he wrote twelve, including *Les Préludes.** Liszt's style is stormy, passionate, and dramatic. The texture of his music is heavy and the harmony rich and chromatic. The various themes within each work are usually derived by transformation of a germinal motive.

I. RICHARD WAGNER (German; 1813–1883). The movement toward alliance of music with the other arts reached a culmination in Wagner's music dramas, in which literary, theatrical, and musical elements are united. Literary and theatrical elements are present, of course, in every opera, but in the music drama they theoretically assume equal importance with the music. The huge Wagnerian orchestra is not merely an accompaniment for singing but is important to the narration; it comments upon the action, reminisces about past events, predicts future happenings, and conveys insight into psychological aspects of the drama by the leitmotiv technique. Portions of the music dramas are often performed as orchestral excerpts. Most of Wagner's operas and music dramas (which include *Lohengrin; Die Meistersinger; Tannhäuser;** the four works which comprise the *Ring of the Nibelungen: Das Rheingold, Die Walküre, Siegfried,* and *Götterdämmerung; Tristan und Isolde;* and *Parsifal*) are continuous, the music not being separated into arias, recitatives, interludes, and other divisions. Wagner's harmony is saturated with chromaticism and employs such frequent modulations that the tonality is often obscured. The melodies are "endless melodies" in which the cadences are thoroughly concealed.

J. GIUSEPPE VERDI (Italian; 1813–1901). Verdi's works are almost exclusively operatic, and his church music, like the *Requiem*, is essentially operatic in style. His *La Traviata, Il Trovatore, Rigoletto, Aïda* * and *Otello* are staples of today's repertory. Rhythm and harmony are much less complex than in most nineteenth-century music, Verdi's emphasis being upon melody. His tunes are long, sweeping lines remarkably attuned to plot and character delineation. The accompaniment is often an unprepossessing orchestral "oomp-pah."

K. CÉSAR FRANCK (Belgian, but lived in France; 1822–1890). Canonic writing and rich Romantic harmony within a framework of expanded Classic forms mark the music of Franck. Cyclical thematic construction is important in the *Symphony in D Minor* and in the *Quintet in F Minor*. His *Symphonic Variations* for piano and orchestra; his *Violin Sonata;* and a number of piano pieces and organ works are part of the standard repertory.

L. BEDŘICH SMETANA (Bohemian; 1824–1884). Smetana was one of the earliest of the ardently nationalistic composers. His most popular opera, *The Bartered Bride*, is based upon a Slavonic subject and saturated with Czech spirit in folk song and dance. In his tone poems, of which *The Moldau* * is best known, he began the use of folk-like themes developed symphonically, a practice which most other nationalistic composers quickly adopted. His *String Quartet in E Minor ("From My Life")* has an autobiographical program.

M. JOHANNES BRAHMS (German; 1833–1897). Brahms' music exhibits none of the programmatic thought common to most late Romantic works. His four symphonies, his concerti, overtures, and chamber works adhere to Classic principles in form, objective expressiveness, and craftsmanlike treatment of themes. However, the melodiousness of his folk-like themes and the harmonic richness and warm sentiment reflected in Brahms' works are characteristically Romantic. Brahms' orchestra is a large one, and his color mixtures are subdued and dark. There are high degrees of rhythmic interest and contrapuntal complexity. His *German Requiem*, many songs and piano pieces, and numerous other compositions constitute an important part of today's repertory.

N. MODESTE MOUSSORGSKY (Russian; 1839–1881). The opera *Boris Godounov*, the suite *Pictures at an Exhibition* (written for piano but transcribed for orchestra by Ravel and others), and the tone poem *Night on the Bare Mountain* * (often called *Night on Bald Mountain;* completed and orchestrated by Rimsky-Korsakov) reveal the characteristic traits of Moussorgsky's style. His melodies are styled after those of Russian folk and religious music, the inflections imitating those of speech. The dramatic treatment is objective and realistic, and the harmony is sometimes harsh where demanded by the program.

O. PETER ILICH TCHAIKOVSKY (Russian; 1840–1893). Not all of Tchaikovsky's works are programmatic but all are subjective and emotional, contrasting moods of serenity, dejection, animation, resignation, and triumph. His symphonies, including the well-known *No. 6 ("Pathétique")* and concerti, among them the familiar *Piano Concerto in B-flat Minor,* adhere loosely to Classic forms. An expanded sonata-allegro design is used in *Romeo and Juliet,** which Tchaikovsky called a "fantasy overture." The *Marche Slave, Nutcracker Suite,* and *1812 Overture,* all orchestral pieces, are part of the popular concert repertory. Tchaikovsky's melodies, melting or bold but always prominent, often are presented by wind instruments. His colorful orchestration uses strikingly contrasting units of string, woodwind, or brass sounds.

P. ANTONÍN DVOŘÁK (Bohemian; 1841–1904). Lively dance rhythms and attractive folk-like melodies permeate Dvořák's music. Themes in the well-known *Symphony No. 5 ("From the New World")** were patterned after American Indian and Negro tunes, although Dvořák's Bohemian temperament is not altogether absent. His symphonies, concerti, and chamber music are shaped in expanded Classic forms, and many are cyclic. Among Dvořák's works in the modern repertory are a concerto for violin and one for cello, the *String Quartet in F Major,* two sets of *Slavonic Dances,* and the symphonies.

Q. EDVARD GRIEG (Norwegian; 1843–1907). Grieg's *Piano Concerto in A Minor* is one of the staples of the popular concert repertory, and the two suites made from his incidental music for *Peer Gynt* are also well known. These works as well as his many songs and piano pieces are influenced by Norwegian folk idiom. Most of Grieg's compositions employ the smaller forms (ternary and rondo structures) and create an impression of archaism through the use of modal melodies and harmonies.

R. NICOLAI RIMSKY-KORSAKOV (Russian; 1844–1908). The rich harmony and Russian flavor of Rimsky-Korsakov's music result in part from the combined use of chromatic harmony with minor-sounding modes peculiar to Russian liturgical music. His *Capriccio Espagnol, Scheherazade,* and *Russian Easter Overture* as well as his operas and symphonies, which are less frequently heard today, have brilliantly colorful orchestrations in which wind and percussion instruments are used with a prominence unusual in the nineteenth century.

S. GIACOMO PUCCINI (Italian; 1858–1924). Puccini's *verismo* (realistic) operas, which include *La Bohème, Tosca,* and *Madame Butterfly,* deal with everyday human characters who have been placed in believable dramatic situations. The melodies are broad and sweetly lyric, the harmonies are rich, and the orchestra is used with more colorful effect than is usual in operas.

T. GUSTAV MAHLER (Bohemian, but lived in Germany and the U.S.A.; 1860–

1911). Mahler was one of the last composer-conductors in the German romantic tradition. His highly emotional, frequently subjective music—sometimes starkly dramatic and sometimes warmly melodious—usually requires a greatly augmented orchestra. Among his better known works are the first of the nine symphonies; a song cycle with orchestra, *Das Lied von der Erde*; and *Kindertotenlieder*.

III. Additional listening suggestions

A. CHORAL MUSIC

1. Luigi Cherubini (Italian; 1760–1842): *Requiem in C Minor*
2. Gabriel Fauré (French; 1845–1924): *Requiem*

B. OPERA AND OPERETTA

1. Giacomo Meyerbeer (German; 1791–1864): *L'Africaine*
2. Gaetano Donizetti (Italian; 1797–1848): *Lucia di Lammermoor*
3. Vincenzo Bellini (Italian; 1801–1835): *Norma*
4. Mikhail Glinka (Russian; 1804–1857): *A Life for the Czar*
5. Charles Gounod (French; 1818–1893): *Faust*
6. Jacques Offenbach (German, but lived in France; 1819–1880): *Tales of Hoffmann*
7. Johann Strauss (Austrian; 1825–1899): *Die Fledermaus*
8. Alexander Borodin (Russian; 1833–1887): *Prince Igor*
9. Camille Saint-Saëns (French; 1835–1921): *Samson and Delilah*
10. Georges Bizet (French; 1838–1875): *Carmen*
11. Jules Massenet (French; 1842–1912): *Manon*
12. Arthur S. Sullivan (English; 1842–1900) and
    William S. Gilbert (English; 1836–1911): *The Mikado*
13. Engelbert Humperdinck (German; 1854–1921): *Hansel and Gretel*
14. Ruggiero Leoncavallo (Italian; 1858–1919): *I Pagliacci*
15. Pietro Mascagni (Italian; 1863–1945): *Cavalleria Rusticana*

C. SYMPHONIC MUSIC

1. Anton Bruckner (Austrian; 1824–1896): *Symphony No. 4 in E-flat*
2. Mily Balakirev (Russian; 1837–1910): *Tamar*
3. Vincent d'Indy (French; 1851–1931): *Symphony on a French Mountain Air*
4. Ernest Chausson (French; 1855–1899): *Poème for Violin and Orchestra*
5. Sir Edward Elgar (English; 1857–1934): *Enigma Variations*
6. Edward MacDowell (American; 1861–1908): *Suite No. 2, ("Indian")*
7. Alexander Glazunov (Russian; 1865–1936): *Violin Concerto in A Minor*
8. Paul Dukas (French; 1865–1935): *The Sorcerer's Apprentice*

D. MISCELLANEOUS MUSIC

1. Nicoló Paganini (Italian; 1782–1840): *Caprices, Op. 1*
2. Hugo Wolf (German; 1860–1903): *Spanisches Liederbuch*
3. Isaac Albéniz (Spanish; 1860–1909): *Iberia*
4. Enrique Granados (Spanish; 1867–1916): *Goyescas*

17

Impressionism

A new style which came to be called Impressionism originated in France late in the nineteenth century as a reaction against realistic programmaticism and formalism.

I. **Characteristics of style.** Although Impressionism is essentially a programmatic style, extramusical ideas are seldom conveyed realistically. Imitation of sounds and movements are foreign to Impressionism, which tends to allude rather than to state, to suggest rather than to describe, to sketch rather than to photograph, and to symbolize rather than to define. Favorite extramusical subjects include the sea, clouds, moonlight, exotic landscapes, and other nature scenes.

A. PERFORMANCE MEDIA. The favored performance media are instrumental, and timbre effects are often of paramount importance. The orchestra is usually of the size associated with "woodwinds in threes." A hazy, luminous shimmer is created by such means as muted strings and brasses, delicately handled percussion instruments, limpid and discreet solo woodwinds, and the blending of individual colors rather than of blocks of choir-sound. The many Impressionistic works for piano reflect the same ethereal quality.

B. RHYTHM. The rhythm, indefinite and subtle, attains considerable fluidity by the use of patterns which obscure the feeling of the downbeat and of meters which group five, seven, or eleven beats per bar.

C. MELODY. Melodies are rarely as prominent or well-defined as are the tunes in most other styles. Various scales other than major or minor (particularly the whole-tone scale and the archaic modes) are important in melodic construction. One brief fragment is frequently repeated and sequenced.

D. TEXTURE. The characteristic texture is light and lacy. Chords, often with added tones, move parallel with the melody. Dissonances are often left unresolved. Imitative counterpoint is seldom employed save when fragments of melody are given to different instruments in a process comparable to *pointillism* (a technique of painting in daubs of color rather than in lines).

E. STRUCTURE AND FORMS. The favored forms are the miniature free forms, unified by re-use of a motive. The devices of variation and development are seldom used. The phrases are usually irregular, with cadences concealed, rendering the internal structure deliberately indefinite and vague. Timbre effects and harmonic structures are sometimes used as subjects.

II. Representative composers

A. CLAUDE DEBUSSY (French; 1862–1918). Impressionism is epitomized in the mature works of Debussy, founder and principal exponent of the style. His well-known works include *La Mer, Prelude to the Afternoon of a Faun,** *Nocturnes,* and other orchestral works; a number of piano pieces; the opera, *Pelléas et Mélisande;* a string quartet, and many songs.

B. MAURICE RAVEL (French; 1875–1937). Although Impressionistic elements are important in Ravel's music (especially in his early works), those elements are often mixed with Spanish influences and with a tendency toward such non-Impressionistic features as clear metrical rhythms, easily discerned phrase structure, and strong cadences. The two suites from the music of his ballet, *Daphnis and Chloe;** the *Mother Goose Suite; Boléro;* and *La Valse* exemplify the brilliance of the orchestral sound characteristic of his style. Other well-known works include the *Piano Concerto in G Major,* the *String Quartet in F Major* and a number of compositions for piano.

III. Additional listening suggestions. As a pure style, Impressionism began and ended with Debussy. Features of the style have, however, been adopted by other composers.

A. Frederick Delius (English; 1862–1934): *On Hearing the First Cuckoo in Spring*
B. Alexander Scriabin (Russian; 1872–1915): *Symphony No. 3, ("The Divine Poem")*
C. John Alden Carpenter (American; 1876–1951): *Adventures in a Perambulator*
D. Manuel de Falla (Spanish; 1876–1946): *Nights in the Gardens of Spain*
E. Ottorino Respighi (Italian; 1879–1936): *The Pines of Rome**
F. Charles Griffes (American; 1884–1920): *Roman Sketches*

18

The
Twentieth Century

At the turn of the nineteenth century, Romantic music dissipated into a group of "-isms." Impressionism was a style in itself. Nationalism demanded that the works of one nation's composers sound different from those of another. Individualism required of each composer a unique style. Realism, carried to the extreme, turned the orchestra into a gigantic sound-effects machine.

The revolution in musical styles at the beginning of the twentieth century was in many ways comparable to that which had occurred in the seventeenth century. Many features of the new music were reactions against the old. Tonality was replaced by atonality, metrical rhythm by unmetrical rhythm, tertian harmony by quartal harmony or by harmony derived from the arbitrary scales which replaced the major and minor scales. In addition, timbre effects and chords replaced themes as musical subjects, and dissonance was no longer subservient to consonance.

Because twentieth-century styles are so diverse and profuse that a comprehensive discussion would involve consideration of individual compositions, generalizations, always convenient and always questionable, must be employed here. (Omitted from this discussion is so-called post-Romantic music which is hardly distinguishable in style from that of the late nineteenth century.)

I. **New techniques.** Experimentations with musical materials have led to significant new techniques, particularly in rhythm and tonal organization.

   A. NEW TONAL ORGANIZATIONS. New tonal organizations replace the major and minor scales in melody, harmony, and counterpoint.

      1. ATONALITY. Atonality destroys the traditional gravity toward a tonal center, primarily through application of the tone-row technique.

      2. POLYTONALITY. Polytonality creates two or more tonal centers by simultaneous use of the resources of two or more keys in counterpoint or in polychords.

      3. PANDIATONICISM. In pandiatonic music the tonality of one key is strongly established, but dissonance occurs freely and the conventional relationships between the principal chords are no longer considered.

      4. NEO-MODALITY. In neo-modality the archaic modes are used in a modern harmonic or contrapuntal context.

B. NEW RHYTHMIC PRACTICES. The techniques noted here are important (though not exclusive) to twentieth century music.

      1. POLYMETRICAL RHYTHM. Two or more meters are used simultaneously in polymetrical rhythm.

      2. MIXED METER. Various meters are used in rapid succession in mixed meter. The meter signature sometimes changes with each measure.

      3. POLYRHYTHM. Two or more prominent rhythmic patterns occur simultaneously in polyrhythm.

II. **New attitudes.** Some of the following twentieth century "-isms" indicate sources for extramusical ideas and others denote a modern eclecticism. An eclectic composer synthesizes his own style from elements of several other styles. Each of the "-isms" is a style possessing characteristic techniques.

A. PRIMITIVISM. Primitivism turns to uncivilized cultures of the past and present for extramusical ideas and for melodic and rhythmic patterns. The music may be marked by wild and barbaric dance rhythms and short, chant-like melodic fragments.

    SUGGESTED LISTENING—Stravinsky: *Le Sacre du Printemps (The Rite of Spring).*

B. FUTURISM. Futurism originated in Italy during the second decade of the century. The outstanding features of futuristic music include the replacement of traditional instruments by "noisemakers." For some works a piano is "prepared" by inserting such objects as rubber erasers, coins, and paper clips between the strings. Recent futuristic composers have experimented with sounds produced electronically and performed through tape recording. An early branch of futurism was *machinism* which, through realistic imitation of sounds and movements, glorifies such extramusical subjects as iron foundries, locomotives, automobiles, and subway trains.

    SUGGESTED LISTENING—Ussachevsky: *Piece for Tape Recorder.*

C. EXPRESSIONISM. Expressionism turns for extramusical ideas to intimate subjective emotions and psychological introspections. Use is made of *Sprechstimme*, a declamation in indefinite pitches. The rhythm is usually complex and fluid. The melodies are often atonal, chromatic, and disjunct. The phrases are of irregular length.

    SUGGESTED LISTENING—Schoenberg: *Pierrot Lunaire.*

D. NEO-CLASSICISM. Neo-Classicism is an eclectic style which employs twentieth-century techniques within a framework of eighteenth-century (or earlier) objectivity and formal clarity. Tone colors are used more to emphasize melodic lines than to create expressive effects. Chamber ensembles and orchestras of moderate size are favored, one important neo-Classic ideal being that of economy of means. The melodies are usually lean, terse, and compact. The texture is usually clean and spare, consisting sometimes of only a few contrapuntal lines. Thematic development, variation, and the devices of contrapuntal imitation unify the forms, many of which are those associated with the Baroque and Classic periods.

SUGGESTED LISTENING—Prokofiev: *Classical Symphony*.

E. NEO-ROMANTICISM. Neo-Romanticism is an eclectic style employing twentieth-century techniques with some of the lyric warmth of Romanticism.

SUGGESTED LISTENING—Hanson: *Symphony No. 2, ("Romantic")*.

III. Representative composers

A. RICHARD STRAUSS (German; 1864–1949). Strauss' music is essentially post-Romantic and realistic, although touched by influences of Impressionism and Expressionism. His orchestral works, which include the tone poems *Till Eulenspiegel's Merry Pranks, Death and Transfiguration*, and *Don Quixote*, require a large orchestra of virtuoso players. Realistic sound effects, thematic transformations, dense but brilliantly colored textures, and wide-ranging, bold melodies are characteristic of his style.

B. JEAN SIBELIUS (Finnish; 1865–1957). The major works of Sibelius, orchestral compositions, are post-Romantic in style. Many of them reflect a spirit of Finnish nationalism and are programmatic in nature. Most of his works are cast in original free forms based on variations and transformation of a germinal motive. His first, second, and fourth symphonies and the violin concerto are regularly performed, and his *Finlandia* and *Valse Triste* are in the popular concert repertory.

C. RALPH VAUGHAN WILLIAMS (English; 1872–1958). English folk songs are used as a thematic basis for some of Vaughan Williams' early works, and the modal flavor of early English music is present in many of his mature works. With few exceptions his compositions are harmonically consonant, rhythmically uncomplicated, and structurally clear. Among his important works are *A Sea Symphony* for chorus and orchestra; *Fantasia on a Theme by Tallis* for string orchestra; *Fantasia on "Greensleeves"*; *Hugh the Drover*, an opera; *A London Symphony*; sacred music; and songs.

D. SERGEI RACHMANINOFF (Russian; 1873–1943). The *Piano Concerto No. 2, Rhapsody on a Theme of Paganini*,* and the *Prelude in C-sharp Minor* hold important places in the popular concert repertory. Rachmaninoff's other works are similarly couched in lush post-Romantic harmony.

E. ARNOLD SCHOENBERG (Austrian, and naturalized American; 1874–1951). *Verklärte Nacht* and other early compositions of Schoenberg are in a post-Romantic style. *Pierrot Lunaire* is strongly Expressionistic. The later works are in the atonal style based on composition in the tone row technique he originated. Among his compositions are those mentioned above, *Chamber Symphony No. 2, Five Pieces for Orchestra, Gurrelieder,* and the four string quartets.

F. CHARLES IVES (American; 1874–1954). Ives' compositions are characterized by complicated rhythms, occasional polytonality and atonality, and frequent contrasts between sections of complex counterpoint and sections of simple harmonic writing. Many of his works employ hymn tunes and melodies characteristic of New England. Among his important works are the *Sonata No. 2 for Piano ("Concord, Mass.")* and the *Symphonies Nos. 2 and 3.*

G. ERNEST BLOCH (Swiss, now in U.S.A.; 1880–   ). Many of Bloch's early works are, like *Baal Shem* and *Schelomo,* rhapsodic works of Hebraic influence mixed with elements of Impressionistic and Romantic styles. His later *Sacred Service,* though conceived for use in the temple, is often performed in concert. Since shortly after World War I, Bloch's compositions have been mostly neo-Classic or neo-Romantic. His major compositions include those noted above, *Four Episodes for Piano, Winds, and Strings,* several symphonies, and a number of chamber works.

H. BÉLA BARTÓK (Hungarian; 1881–1945). Bartok's compositions include operas, songs, and choral works, but these are heard less frequently than his instrumental works such as the *Concerto for Orchestra; Music for Strings, Percussion, and Celesta;* the *Concerto for Violin, Concerto for Viola,* and the *Concerto No. 3 for Piano;* the six string quartets; and *Microcosmos* and other piano works. The melodies are usually angular, the texture thin with extensive imitative counterpoint, and the rhythm percussive and often frenzied. In his works, which variously exhibit Primitivism, neo-Classicism, and Expressionism, the music is usually poly- or neo-tonal, but is sometimes atonal.

I. IGOR STRAVINSKY (Russian, now in U.S.A.; 1882–   ). *The Firebird, Petrouchka,** and *Le Sacre du Printemps,* all ballet suites, exhibit the Primitivism of Stravinsky's early works and the brilliant orchestration characteristic of his style. His mature style, neo-Classic and neo-tonal, is dominant in the *Symphony in Three Movements,* the *Concerto in E-flat Major ("Dumbarton Oaks"),* and other later works. Stravinsky's melodies often resemble those of Russian folk songs. The rhythms are complex and powerful. In his recent compositions a modification of the tone-row technique is employed.

J. ALBAN BERG (Austrian; 1885–1935). Berg's important works, *Concerto for Violin and Orchestra;* the string quartets; the *Lyric Suite;* and the operas, *Wozzeck* and *Lulu,* are tone-row compositions. His atonal music is remarkably imbued with a neo-Romantic warmth.

K. SERGE PROKOFIEV (Russian; 1891–1953). Some of Prokofiev's early works, such as the *Scythian Suite,* are influenced by Primitivism and are quite dissonant. Other compositions, such as the *Classical Symphony*, the *Piano Concerto No. 3*, and the *Violin Concerto No. 1* are strongly neo-Classical with overtones of neo-Romanticism. His *Peter and the Wolf* is a popular concert item. Prokofiev's style features polytonality and pan-diatonicism with clear and vital rhythm in a spare texture.

L. WALTER PISTON (American; 1894–   ). Piston's compositions are almost exclusively absolute music, although his best-known work, a suite from the ballet, *The Incredible Flutist*, is programmatic. Piston's music combines a high degree of imitation in the contrapuntal texture with sharply accented rhythmic patterns. His music is tonal but quite dissonant. Among his significant compositions are the *Symphony No. 3*, the *Symphony No. 4*, and many chamber works.

M. PAUL HINDEMITH (German; 1895–   ). Although a strong neo-Classic spirit is found in most of the works of Hindemith, some of his early compositions, such as the symphony (taken from his opera) *Mathis der Maler*, are neo-Romantically programmatic. Hindemith has supplied sonatas for such instruments as English horn, bassoon, and trombone as well as a number of instruction pieces for students and songs for children. Among his compositions are a *Symphony in E-flat Major; Noblissima Visione*; sonatas for piano and violin; song cycles; and piano works including *Ludus Tonalis*. Imitative counterpoint is important in Hindemith's textures and, although there are atonal moments, most of his music is tonal.

N. HOWARD HANSON (American; 1896–   ). Hanson's style, neo-Romantic, lyric, and richly textured, is based on modal melodies and uses tertian and quartal harmony. His fairly regular, driving rhythms sometimes reveal the influence of jazz. Dissonance, used sparingly, is usually resolved. His *Symphony No. 2, Cherubic Hymn* for chorus and orchestra, and *Chorale* and *Alleluia* for band, are among his better known works.

O. VIRGIL THOMSON (American; 1896–   ). Thomson's music is styled with relative simplicity, clear textures, and uncomplicated rhythm. Many of his melodies are patterned after hymn tunes and American folk songs. His compositions include the opera *Four Saints in Three Acts*; a large number of chamber works; *The Plow that Broke the Plains*, and other music for motion pictures; songs; and choral works.

P. ROGER SESSIONS (American; 1896–   ). Sessions' style is one of rhythmic complexity, structural originality, contrapuntal texture which is often quite dissonant, and wide-ranging melodies. Included among his better known works are the *Sonata No. 2 for Piano* and *The Black Maskers*, a suite of incidental music.

Q. ROY HARRIS (American; 1898–   ). Harris often employs melodies in the nature of hymns and American folk songs. The contrapuntal textures, generally rather consonant, sometimes are polytonal. Among Harris' better known works, many of which are free forms, is his *Symphony No. 3*.

R. AARON COPLAND (American; 1900–   ). Evidences of conscious Americanism are evident in such Copland works as the ballets—*Billy the Kid,** *Appalachian Spring,* and *Rodeo*—as well as in *A Lincoln Portrait,* a piece for narrator and orchestra. His more recent works tend toward a more international neo-Classicism. Fundamentally tonal and diatonic, Copland's music is usually not extremely dissonant. The textures are homophonic, although his chamber works are more polyphonic. Neo-tonal writing in quartal harmony prevails, and the rhythmic idioms of jazz and modern dance are sometimes prominent.

S. SAMUEL BARBER (American; 1910–   ). Barber's style is essentially neo-Romantic, quite chromatic and sometimes rather dissonant. The rhythm is fairly regular and the characteristic texture is contrapuntal. His recorded works include *Adagio for Strings,* the opera *Vanessa,* two symphonies, several chamber works, and songs.

IV. Additional listening suggestions

A. OPERA

1. Zoltán Kodály (Hungarian; 1882–   ): *Hary Janos*
2. Douglas Moore (American; 1893–   ): *The Devil and Daniel Webster*
3. George Gershwin (American; 1898–1937): *Porgy and Bess*
4. Kurt Weill (German-American; 1900–1950): *The Threepenny Opera*
5. Ernst Křenek (German-American; 1900–   ): *Jonny Spielt Auf*
6. Gian-Carlo Menotti (Italian-American; 1911–   ): *The Consul*

B. CHORAL WORKS

1. Arthur Honegger (French; 1892–1955): *King David*
2. Carl Orff (Hungarian; 1895–   ): *Carmina Burana*
3. Randall Thompson (American; 1899–   ): *Testament of Freedom*
4. William Walton (English; 1902–   ): *Belshazzar's Feast*
5. Norman Dello Joio (American; 1913–   ): *Psalm of David*
6. Benjamin Britten (English; 1913–   ): *A Ceremony of Carols*

C. ORCHESTRAL WORKS

1. Albert Roussel (French; 1869–1937): *Bacchus et Ariane*
2. Gustav Holst (English; 1874–1934): *The Planets*
3. Reinhold Glière (Russian; 1875–1956): *Ilya Murometz*
4. Ernst von Dohnányi (Hungarian, now in U.S.A.; 1877–   ): *Variations on a Nursery Theme*
5. Georges Enesco (Roumanian; 1881–1955): *Roumanian Rhapsodies*
6. Wallingford Riegger (American; 1885–   ): *Symphony No. 3*
7. Deems Taylor (American; 1885–   ): *Through the Looking Glass*
8. Bohuslav Martinu (Czech; 1890–   ): *Concerto Grosso (1938)*
9. Jacques Ibert (French; 1890–   ): *Escales*
10. Ferde Grofé (American; 1892–   ): *Grand Canyon Suite*
11. Darius Milhaud (French; 1892–   ): *Suite Provençale*

12. Francis Poulenc (French; 1899–   ): *Les Biches (1924)*
13. Aram Khachaturian (Armenian; 1903–   ): *Gayne (Ballet Suites Nos. 1 and 2)*
14. Dmitri Shostakovitch (Russian; 1906–   ): *Concerto for Piano*
15. Paul Creston (American; 1906–   ): *Invocation and Dance*
16. William Schuman (American; 1910–   ): *Symphony for Strings*
17. Alan Hovhaness (American; 1911–   ): *Prelude and Quadruple Fugue*
18. David Diamond (American; 1915–   ): *Rounds for String Orchestra*
19. Peter Mennin (American; 1923–   ): *Symphony No. 3*

D. CHAMBER MUSIC

1. Hector Villa-Lobos (Brazilian; 1887–   ): *Bachianas Brasileiras No. 9*
2. Anton Webern (Austrian; 1883–1945): *Five Movements for String Quartet*
3. Edgar Varèse (French-American; 1885–   ): *Ionization*
4. Bernard Rogers (American; 1893–   ): *Soliloquy for Flute and Strings*
5. Quincy Porter (American; 1897–   ): *Music for Strings*

E. MISCELLANEOUS

1. Erik Satie (French; 1866–1925): *Three Pieces in the Shape of a Pear*
2. Vincent Persichetti (American; 1915–   ): *Divertimento for Band*

Line Scores
for Listening

Johann Sebastian Bach

Cantata No. 4, "Christ Lag in Todesbanden"

Sinfonia

Excerpt from Verse I

"Christ lay in the bonds of Death, sacrificed for our sins. He has arisen and brought us life. So let us be joyful and praise God in our gratitude and let us sing Hallelujah."

Verse II

"No one could force Death away, burdened as we were by sins. No innocence was there to find. Thus Death overpowered us and kept us in his bonds. Hallelujah."

Phrase 2

kein Un - schuld war _____ zu fin -

ALTO

kein Un-schuld war zu fin - - -

Phrase 3

den.

continuo

Da - von kam _____ der Tod,

ALTO

den.

Da-von kam der

30

der Tod, der Tod so bald,

Phrase 4

und

Tod, der Tod so bald,

continuo

nahm ü - - ber uns _____ Ge - walt,

ALTO

und nahm ü - - - - ber uns Ge - walt,

Phrase 5

40

continuo

hielt uns in sei - nem

ALTO

hielt uns in sei - - nem Reich ge-

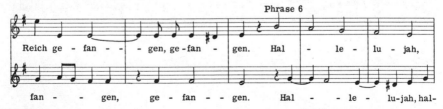

Phrase 6

Reich ge - fan - - gen, ge -fan - gen. Hal - le - lu - jah,

fan - gen, ge - fan - gen. Hal - le - lu-jah, hal-

50

hal - - le - lu - jah, hal - - le - - lu - jah, hal -

- le - - lu - jah, hal - le - - lu - jah, hal -

le - lu - jah!   continuo

le - lu - jah!

Verse III

"Christ Jesus, God's Son, came to our aid, and He removed our sins from us and so Death itself. All his might and power taken, Death lost his sting forever. Hallelujah."

und   hat   die   Sün - de

weg-ge - tan,

da - mit   dem

Tod   ge - - nom - - - men

all' sein Recht   und   sein'   Ge - walt,

da   blei - bet   nichts   denn Tod's - - -

- - ge - stalt,

den

Stach'l hat   er   ver - lo - ren.

TENOR Phrase 6

continuo

Hal - le - lu - jah, hal-le-lu- jah, hal-le - lu - jah,_____ hal-le-lu-

continuo

jah, hal - - - - - - - le - lu-jah!

Excerpt from Verse IV

"It was a wondrous battle when Life and Death fought. Life was victorious and conquered Death forever. This the Scripture tells us. As Death destroyed itself, a farce is all that is left. Hallelujah."

SOPRANO Phrase 2

Da Tod und   Le - ben run -

TENOR   Phrase 1

Es   war   ein wun-der - li - cher Krieg, ein wun - - - - der - li - cher

Verse V

"Here is the real Lamb of God who lovingly suffered for us high on the cross. His blood marks the door of our faith to keep Death away, never to harm us again. Hallelujah."

-ten, da - von Gott hat__ ge - bo - - ten,   das

ist hoch an des Kreu-zes Stamm, hoch an_____ des_____ Kreu -

- - zes, des Kreu-zes Stamm in hei - sser Lieb'_____ ge - bra - ten, in

hei - sser Lieb___ ge - bra - ten,   das Blut zeich-net,   das Blut zeich-net,

zeich - - net un-ser Tür.

das Blut zeich - - - net un -ser Tür, das hält_____ der Glaub'___ dem

Verse VI

"We celebrate this holy feast with joy and jubilation. The rays of His sun shine into our heart, His grace replacing our sins forever. Hallelujah."

Verse VII

"We eat and live well in the proper Easter spirit, and the old and evil will not again touch us who are blessed with His grace. Christ will be our bread alone and will nourish our soul. Our faith will live no other way. Hallelujah."

Johann Sebastian Bach

Fugue in C Minor from the *Well-Tempered Clavichord, Vol. I, No. 2*

Subject

Episode

Subject

Episode

Answer

Episode

Johann Sebastian Bach

Suite No. 2 in B Minor for Flute and Strings

Excerpts from Overture ("French").

Ex. 1

[Grave]

Ex. 2

[Allegro] Fugue

Ex. 3

Rondeau (ABACA)

Sarabande: Binary form.

Bourrée I: Binary form.

Bourrée II: Binary form.

Bourrée I D.C.

Polonaise: Binary form.

Polonaise D.C.

Minuet: Binary form.

[Allegretto]

Badinerie: Binary form.

[Allegro]

Ludwig van Beethoven

Symphony No. 5 in C Minor

First Movement: Sonata-allegro form.

Second Movement: Free variations on two themes.

(Theme II repeated)

Transition

horns, oboes

violins

Variation I (Theme I)

cresc. vlas, bn, clar   violas, celli

violins

cresc.

flute

cresc.   cresc.   violins

cresc.   flute   Theme II

clarinets, bassoons

violins   full orch.   trpts, horns, oboes

Transition

violins

Variation II (Theme I)

cresc.

violas, celli

violins

celli, basses

(Repeated chords in orchestra)

Third Movement: Scherzo with trio.

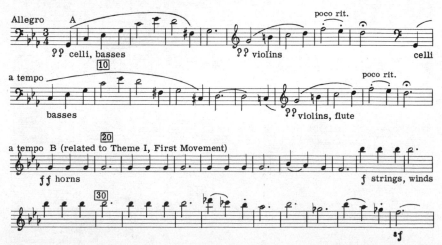

Fourth Movement: Sonata-allegro form.

Exposition: Theme I (A)

f winds, brass

ff

full orch. sf

sf   sf   sf

(End of Theme I, B)

ff bassoons   p horns   p winds

(Theme II, accomp. motive)

f winds, strings   full orch.

(Theme I, B)

p   f strings

horns, oboe, flute   p strings

(Theme II, accomp. motive)

f strings, winds   full orch.   p strings   cresc.

Sempre piu allegro

Presto (Closing theme)

fp vlns

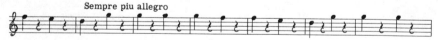

fp violins, winds   fp   fp

fp   cresc.

Johannes Brahms

Sonata in D Minor for Violin and Piano, Op. 108

First Movement: Sonata-allegro form.

Second Movement: Sonatina form.

Exposition: Theme I
Adagio

Third Movement: ABA Coda.

Fourth Movement: Modified sonata-allegro form.

Antonin Dvořák

Symphony No. 5 in E Minor, "From the New World"

First Movement: Sonata-allegro form.

(Theme I)

fz violins   fz   fz   fz   410

(Theme I, octave higher)   420

fz violins fz fz   fz   fz fz   fz

(continues octave higher)   (Theme I)

fz   fz

430   (Theme I)

fz   ff

440   (octave higher)

trbns, low strings   violins

Second Movement: Ternary form.

Largo   A Introduction

ppp brass, clars, bssns   cresc.   f dim. ppp strings

a   10

p English horn

pp   cresc. f   dim.

20

clarinets   winds   cresc. fz

pp

b

ff   dim.   ppp   strings

30

a

p English horn

Third Movement: Scherzo with trio.

Fourth Movement: Sonata-allegro form.

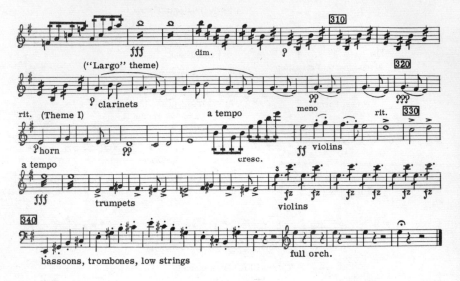

("Largo" theme)
dim.
ƒƒƒ
clarinets
rit. (Theme I)
a tempo
meno
rit.
horn
violins
cresc.
a tempo
trumpets
violins
ƒƒƒ
bassoons, trombones, low strings
full orch.

Gregorian Chant

Dies Irae: Sequence from the *Requiem Mass*

First Verse. Day of wrath, day of judgment,
When the earth dissolves in ashes:
So say David and Sibyl.

Di-es i-rae, di-es il-la, Sol-vet sae-clum in fa-vil-la:

Tes-te Da-vid cum Si-byl-la.

Sanctus from the *Requiem Mass*

Holy, Holy, Holy Lord God of Hosts.
Heaven and earth are full of Thy glory.
Hosanna in the highest.
Blessed is He who comes in the name of the Lord.
Hosanna in the highest.

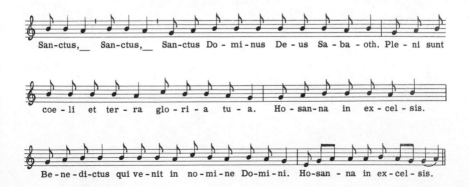

San-ctus,__ San-ctus,__ San-ctus Do - mi-nus De - us Sa - ba - oth. Ple - ni sunt

coe - li et ter - ra glo - ri - a tu - a. Ho - san-na in ex - cel - sis.

Be - ne - di-ctus qui ve - nit in no - mi - ne Do-mi-ni. Ho-san - na in ex-cel-sis.

Lumen ad Revelationem—Nunc Dimittis

(Sung during the distribution of candles on the Feast of the Purification, February 2nd)

> A light of revelation to the Gentiles:
> and glory for Thy people Israel.
>
> Now O Lord Thou dost dismiss Thy servant,
> according to Thy word, in peace.

Refrain

Lu - men ad re - ve - la - ti - on - em gen-ti - um: et___ glo-ri - am ple-bis tu-ae Is-ra-el.

Eighth Psalm Tone

Nunc di - mittis servum tu - um, Do-mi-ne, secundum verbum tu - um in pa - ce.

George Frederick Handel

Messiah

No. 44: Chorus, "Hallelujah"

    Messiah is composed of fifty-three arias, recitatives, choruses, and orchestral numbers. This chorus, one of twenty, is scored for a four-part chorus and orchestra.

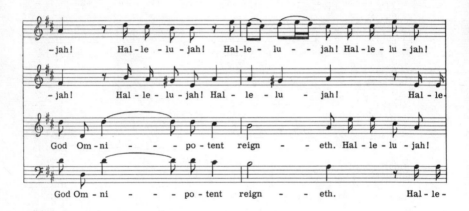

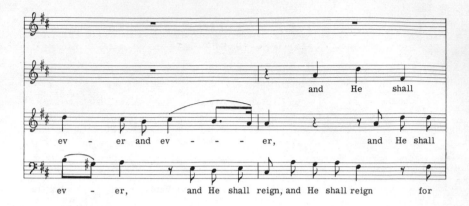

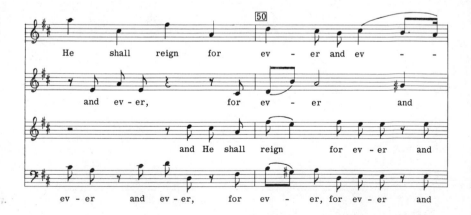

and Lord of Lords,

-lu-jah! For ev-er and ev-er. Hal-le-lu-jah! Hal-le-

-lu-jah! For ev-er and ev-er. Hal-le-lu-jah! Hal-le-

-lu-jah! For ev-er and ev-er. Hal-le-lu-jah! Hal-le-

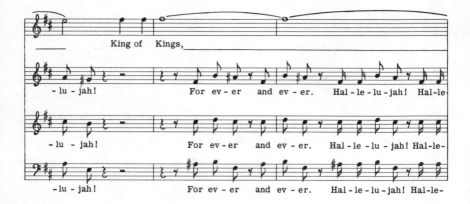

King of Kings,

-lu-jah! For ev-er and ev-er. Hal-le-lu-jah! Hal-le-

-lu-jah! For ev-er and ev-er. Hal-le-lu-jah! Hal-le-

-lu-jah! For ev-er and ev-er. Hal-le-lu-jah! Hal-le-

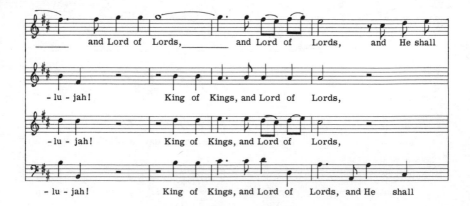

and Lord of Lords, and Lord of Lords, and He shall

-lu-jah! King of Kings, and Lord of Lords,

-lu-jah! King of Kings, and Lord of Lords,

-lu-jah! King of Kings, and Lord of Lords, and He shall

No. 45: Aria, "I know that my Redeemer liveth."

Messiah contains sixteen arias for soprano, alto, tenor, and bass. This aria is one of four for soprano.

flesh   shall   I   see   God,   yet in my flesh_____   shall

I   see   God, shall   I   see   God.   I   know that   my Re - deem - er

violins   liv - eth.   For now is   Christ ris-en

violins   from the   dead,   the   first -

fruits of   them that sleep,_____   of them   that sleep,   the

violins   first - - fruits of   them   that   sleep.

For   now is   Christ ris - en,   for   now is   Christ

violins   ris - en from   the   dead,   the   first - fruits of

Adagio   a tempo & full orchestra   them, of   them   that sleep.

Franz Joseph Haydn

Symphony No. 94 in G Major, "Surprise"

Third Movement: Theme and Variations.

Wolfgang Amadeus Mozart

"Eine Kleine Nachtmusik," Serenade for Strings, K. 525

First Movement: Sonatina form.

Second Movement: Romance (Rondo—ABACA).

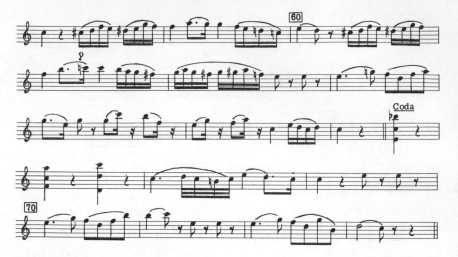

Third Movement: Menuetto-trio.

Finale: Sonata-allegro form.

Exposition: Theme I
Allegro

176   WOLFGANG AMADEUS MOZART

Wolfgang Amadeus Mozart

The Marriage of Figaro

From Act I

The plot of the opera revolves about the intrigues of Count Almaviva with Susanna, the Countess's maid. The Count's valet, Figaro, who is about to be married to Susanna, discovers that she is the object of the Count's affections, and is determined to use his wits to thwart him.

As the first scene opens, Figaro is seen measuring the floor of a partially furnished room, while Susanna, before a mirror, tries on a hat.

No. 1   Duet: Figaro and Susanna. (English translation on p. 185.)

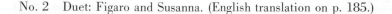

In the secco recitative that follows, Susanna inquires of Figaro why he is measuring the room. Figaro replies that he is trying to discover the best place in the room for the bed the Count has given them as a wedding present. Susanna protests that she does not want this room; she has reasons he doesn't know. Figaro cannot understand why she will not have it, as it is the best room of the castle.

No. 2   Duet: Figaro and Susanna. (English translation on p. 185.)

In the next dialogue, in secco recitative, Susanna discloses to Figaro that the Count has eyes for none other than his little Susanna. For this reason, she says, he has given them this room, and her a handsome dowry. Figaro is incredulous. At this moment the Countess's bell rings, and Susanna leaves the room. Figaro then begins to awaken to the Count's purpose, and he vows that his plans shall not succeed.

No. 3   Aria: Figaro. (English translation on p. 186.)

le suo-ne - rò, si,   le suo-ne-rò, si,   le suo-ne-rò.

oboe

Se vuol ve - ni - re   nel-la mia sco-la,   la ca - pri - o - la

le in-se - gne - rò,   se vuol ve-ni - re   nel - la mia sco-la,   la ca - pri -

- o - la   le in - se-gne-rò, si,   le in - se - gne - rò, si,   le in - se -gne-

- rò.   Sa -prò,   sa-

violins

- prò,   sa - prò   sa - prò   sa -

violins

prò   ma pia - no,_____   pia-no, pia - no,

pia - no, pia - no, pia - no,   pia - no,   violins

me-gl'ogni arca - no dis-si - mu - lan - do sco-prir po-trò.   Presto   L'ar-te scher-

- men-do, l'ar te a-do-pran-do, di qua pun-gnen-do, di la scher-zan-do, tut - te le

macchine ro -ve-scie-rò, ro - ve - scie - rò.   L'ar-te scher-

-men-do, l'ar - te a-do-pran-do, di qua pun-gnen-do, di là scher-zan-do, tut - te le

mac - chi-ne ro - ve-scie - rò,   tut - te le macchine ro - ve - scie - rò, tut - te le mac-chi-ne ro - ve-scie - rò, ro - ve-scie - rò, ro - ve - scie-rò.

Tempo I

Se vuol bal-la - re, si - gnor Con - ti - no,   se vuol bal - la - re, si-gnor Con-

- ti - no,   il chi - tar - ri - no le   suo - ne - rò,   il chi - tar -

- ri - no le suo-ne - rò, si,   le suo - ne - rò, si,   le suo-ne - rò.

Presto

violins

No. 1   Duet

FIG.	Five, ten, twenty, thirty, thirty-six, forty-three.
SUS.	Yes, I am truly contented, it seems in truth just made for me.
	Please look here, my dearest Figaro, look one moment at my hat.
FIG.	Yes, my love, it is very beautiful, seems in truth just made for you.
SUS.	Ah, the day of the marriage approaches.
AND FIG.	Ah, how sweet to me is my tender spouse.

This ⎰ my ⎱ beautiful, charming little hat, which Susanna made herself.
⎩ your ⎭

No. 2   Duet

FIG.	Supposing the countess one evening should want you—
	Ding, ding, in two paces you'll be at her side.
	Or then, on occasion, if his lordship should want me,
	Dong, dong, in three steps I am there at his side.
SUS.	So if one morning the dearest count should call you,
	And send you three miles away,
	Ding, ding, dong, dong, to my door the devil will bring him;
	He's here in just three leaps.
FIG.	Susanna, hush, hush!
SUS.	Now listen—
FIG.	Tell me quickly!
SUS.	If you want to hear it, discard your suspicion, which makes me sad.
FIG.	Yes, I want to hear it.
	My doubt and suspicion make my heart cold!

No. 3   Aria

FIG.   If you wish to dance, your lordship,
My guitar will play the tune, yes, play the tune.
If you wish to come to my school,
I will teach you to cut capers, yes, I'll teach you.
I know how—but softly!
I must be cautious; one unguarded word may mar my plans.
Cleverly hiding, busily doing,
My time awaiting while you are wooing,
All of your intrigue I will overcome.
If you wish to dance, your lordship,
My guitar will play the tune, yes, play the tune!

Henry Purcell

"Dido's Lament" from *Dido and Aeneas*

Recitative: Thy hand, Belinda; darkness shades me:
　　　　　On thy bosom let me rest!
　　　　　More I would, but Death invades me:
　　　　　Death is now a welcome guest!

187

Franz Schubert

Der Erlkönig (Text by Johann Wolfgang von Goethe)

Schnell (Allegro)

rei - tet so spät durch Nacht und Wind? Es ist der Va - ter mit sei - nem Kind; er hat den Kna - ben wohl in dem Arm, er fasst ihn si - cher, er hält ihn warm. Mein Sohn, was birgst du so bang dein Ge- -sicht? Siehst, Va - ter, du den Erl-kö - nig nicht? den

Er - len - kö - nig mit Kron' und Schweif? Mein Sohn, es ist ein

Ne - bel - streif. "Du lie - bes Kind, komm', geh' mit

mir! gar schö - ne Spie - le spiel' ich mit dir; manch' bun - te

Blu - men sind an dem Strand; mei-ne Mut-ter hat manch' gül - den Ge-

-wand." Mein Va - ter, mein Va - ter, und hö - rest du nicht, was

Erl - len - kö - nig mir lei - se ver -spricht? Sei ru - hig, blei - be

ru - hig, mein Kind; in dür - ren Blät - tern säu -selt der Wind.

"Willst, fei - ner Kna - be, du mit mir geh'n? mei-ne Töch-ter sol - len dich

war - ten schön; mei-ne Töch - ter füh - ren den nächt - li -chen Reih'n und

wie - gen und tan-zen und sin - gen dich ein, sie wie-gen und tan-zen und

sin - gen dich ein." Mein Va - ter, mein Va - ter, und siehst du nicht

dort Erl - kö -nigs Töch - ter am dü - stern Ort? Mein Sohn, mein

Sohn, ich seh' es ge - nau, es schei -nen die al - ten Wei - den so grau.

piano

"Ich lie - be dich, mich

reizt dei - ne schö - ne Ge - stalt, und bist du nicht wil - lig, so brauch' ich Ge-

-walt." Mein Va - ter, mein Va - ter, jetzt fasst er mich an! Erl - kö - nig

hat mir ein Leid's ge - tan!   Dem Va - ter grau - set's, er

rei - tet ge - schwind, er hält in Ar - men das äch - zen - de Kind,

er - reicht den Hof mit Müh und Not;

Recit.   piano

in sei-nen Ar - men das Kind war tot.

The Erl King

Who gallops so late through night and wind?
It is the father with his child.
He has the boy so safe in his arm;
He clasps him tightly, he keeps him warm.

My son, in terror why hide you your face?
Oh father, see the Erl King is near,
The Erl King I fear, with crown and robe!
My son, it is a cloud of mist.

"My lovely child, come, go with me!
Such pleasant games I'll play with you.
So many flowers are blooming there,
And my mother has many golden robes for you!"

My father, my father, now truly you hear
What the Erl King whispers so softly to me?
Be quiet, please be quiet, my child;
'Tis but the dead leaves stirred by the wind.

"My lovely boy, will you go with me?
My fair daughters will wait on you.
My fair daughters dance in the revels all night.
They'll sing and they'll dance and they'll rock you to sleep;
They'll sing and they'll dance and they'll rock you to sleep!"

My father, my father, and do you not see
The Erl King's daughters in that dark spot?
My son, my son, I see very well,
It is only the old willows so gray!

"I love you, child, your beautiful form inflames me!
And if you're not willing, I must then use force!"

My father, my father, he now grasps my arm,
The Erl King has seized me, his grasp hurts me!"

The father shudders. He rides like the wind,
The child held in his arms, the sick, dying child.
He reaches home with fear and dread;
And in his arms, the child was dead.

Franz Schubert

Der Wanderer   (Text by George Philipp Schmidt)

Sehr langsam (Adagio)

Ich kom-me vom Ge-bir-ge her,   es dampft das Tal,

es braust das Meer,   es braust das Meer.   Ich wand-le

still, bin we-nig froh,   und im-mer fragt der Seuf - zer:

wo? im - - mer wo?   Die Son - ne dünkt mich hier so_ kalt, die

Blü - - te welk,   das Le - ben alt, und was sie re - - den,

lee - - rer Schall, ich bin ein Fremd - ling ü - ber-all.   Wo

bist du,   wo bist du,   mein ge- lieb - tes Land?   ge - sucht,_ ge -

The Wanderer

I come here from my highland home.
The vale is dim, the sea does roar.
I wander on with little joy,
And always asks my sighing, "Where?" always "Where?"
The sun to me seems to be so cold,
The flowers are faded and life is old.
The language seems an empty shell,
I feel a stranger ev'rywhere.

Where art thou, where art thou, my beloved land?
In hope, I seek but never know.
That land, that land where hope is green,
The land where roses bloom for me;
Where walk the friends so dear to me,
Where all my dead will live again,
That land where they speak my language,
O land, where art thou?

I wander on with little joy,
And always asks my sighing, "Where?" always "Where?"
In ghostly voice the answer comes:
"There, where thou art not, there is thy fate!"

Giuseppe Verdi

Aida

Act IV, Scene II

For this scene, the last of the opera, the stage is divided into two levels. Above is the temple of Vulcan, resplendent in gold; below is the vault in which Radames, Egyptian general, has been sentenced to be buried alive. Radames has incurred a false charge of treason as a result of his love for Aida, an Ethiopian princess who is a captive of the Egyptians.

Upon entering the tomb, Radames discovers Aida concealed there, prepared to die with him. The priests and priestesses above in the temple invoke the almighty Fthà as Aida and Radames bid farewell to the world and die in each other's arms. Amneris, the Egyptian princess who has loved Radames in vain, prays to Isis for his soul.

Translation:

RADAMES: The fatal stone upon me now is closing.
            Behold the tomb engulfs me.
            Nevermore shall I behold the light,
            Nor shall I see Aida . . .
            Aida, where are you now?
            Whatever happens, may you be happy.
            May my awful doom never reach your gentle ear.
            What groan was that?
            It is a phantom . . . a vision,
            No, the form is human . . .
            Heaven! Aida!

AIDA: It is I.

RADAMES: You! In this tomb buried!

AIDA: In my heart I saw this frightful sentence.
            Into this tomb that encloses you
            I crept unseen.
            Here, far away from every human glance,
            I desire to die in your embrace.

RADAMES: To die! So pure and lovely!
            To die because you love me,
            In all your flowery beauty to fly forever!
            You whom heaven created for love alone,
            To destroy you was my love so fated!
            No! Not to die!
            I love you too much; you are too lovely!

AIDA: See now where death as an angel
            Radiantly draws near to lead us

To eternal joys above
On wings of gold.
Now see heaven's gates open wide.
There every grief ceases, ecstasy begins,
And there is immortal love.

CHORUS: Almighty Fthà, who animates the spirit of the world,
          Ah! Ah! We invoke thee, we invoke thee!
AIDA: Sorrowful chant!
RADAMES: It is the supplication of the priests.
AIDA: It is the hymn for our death.
RADAMES: (trying to move the stone) Can not my strong arms move this fatal stone?
AIDA: Now all hope on earth for us is finished.
RADAMES: It is true! It is true!
AIDA: Farewell, O earth, farewell, O vale of sorrow,
          Brief dream destined to end in grief.
          For us heaven opens,
          Heaven with endless morn.
          There will be the light of the eternal day.
RADAMES: Farewell, O earth, (etc.)
CHORUS: Almighty Fthà, we invoke thee, we invoke thee.
AIDA AND
RADAMES: Farewell, O earth, (etc.)
AMNERIS: Peace, I implore, adored Radames.
          May Isis be appeased, may Isis open heaven.
          Peace, I implore! Peace, peace!

Richard Wagner

Overture to *Tannhäuser*

In this overture Wagner depicts the two opposing forces of the opera, spiritual and sensual love. Tannhäuser, the hero of the opera, is torn between his love for the pure and beautiful Elisabeth and the pagan goddess, Venus.

The overture is written in an ABA form. The first and last sections are dominated by the Pilgrims' Chorus, with the middle section given to the Venusberg music.

The titles of the various motives in this overture have been given by various commentators on Wagner's music.

poco accel.

fp

sempre cresc.

140

f   piu *f*   *ff*   *ff*

Tempo I

full orch. *f* "Glorification of Venus" motive

150

f

meno *f*   violins, high winds

160

cresc.   piu *f*   **170**

ff (continues octave higher)   *ff*   *ff*

180 violas

dim.

pp flutes

190

p violins

"Charm of Venus" motive

p   piu *p*   clarinet

200

violins

violins

Abbreviated Analyses

Johann Sebastian Bach

Fugue in C Major from the *Well-Tempered Clavichord, Vol. I, No. 1*

EXPOSITION

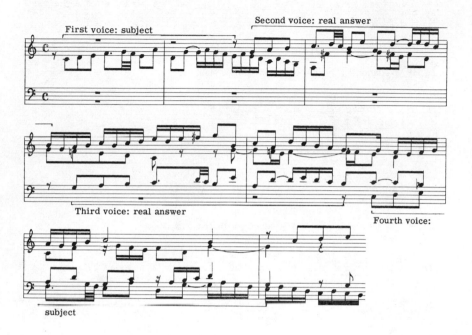

Johann Sebastian Bach

Passacaglia in C Minor for Organ (Twenty variations)

The following examples illustrate the subject of the passacaglia and eight variations selected from the total of twenty. The passacaglia is followed immediately by a four-voice fugue which utilizes as a subject the first four measures of the passacaglia subject.

Ex. 1 Subject.

Ex. 2   Variation I. Syncopation in upper voices.

Ex. 3   Variation VI. Scale-passage accompaniment.

Ex. 4   Variation IX. Bass line ornamented, rhythm varied.

Ex. 5   Variation X. Subject in bass becomes bass of chords accompanying counterpoint in upper voice.

Ex. 6   Variation XI. Subject in upper voice.

Ex. 7 Variation XV. Subject as part of arpeggio line.

Ex. 8 Variation XVII. Rapid counterpoint in upper voices.

Ex. 9 Variation XVIII. New rhythmic figure in upper voices. Subject in bass altered rhythmically.

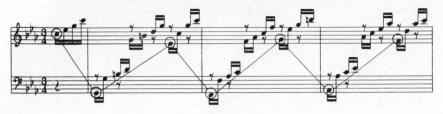

Ludwig van Beethoven

Piano Sonata No. 8 in C Minor, Op. 13 ("Pathétique")

First Movement: Sonata-allegro form.

INTRODUCTION

Ex. 1 Principal motive.

EXPOSITION

Ex. 2 Theme I.

Ex. 3 Theme II.

Ex. 4 Closing theme, beginning.

Ex. 5 Theme I recalled, major key.

DEVELOPMENT

Ex. 6   Principal motive from introduction recalled.

Ex. 7   Theme I developed.

Ex. 8   Theme II developed.

Ex. 9   Theme I developed.

Ex. 10   Close of development.

RECAPITULATION: closely resembles exposition.

CODA

Ex. 11   Principal motive from the introduction recalled.

Ex. 12   Close of coda. Theme I.

Second Movement: Rondo. ABACA coda. (Continuous line score.)

Third Movement: Rondo. ABACABA coda.

Ex. 13

Ex. 14

Ex. 15

Ex. 16

Ex. 17

Ex. 18   CODA. Reference to A, major key.

Frédéric Chopin
Etude in E Major, Op. 10, No. 3

TERNARY FORM: ABA

Ex. 1

Continuation of B. Florid passages of great technical difficulty in animated tempo (five phrases).

Ex. 2

Aaron Copland

Street Scene from *Billy the Kid*

The Street Scene, the first scene of the ballet, follows a slow introduction. The setting is of a typical Western frontier town. Crossing the street are girls, women, and cowboys, some on horseback. Examples 1, 2, 3, 4, and 5 are tunes used to portray the sauntering groups.

Ex. 1

Ex. 2

Ex. 3

Ex. 4

Examples 1 and 2 are heard again.

Ex. 5

Billy the Kid. Copyright 1941 by Hawkes and Son (London) Ltd. Used by permission of Boosey and Hawkes Inc.

Attention then shifts to a troupe of Mexican women who do a *jarabe* (a lively Mexican dance):

Ex. 6

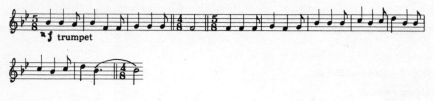

Two drunks appear:

Ex. 7

This tune is repeated again and again with greater force as the drunks begin a quarrel which quickly becomes ugly. Guns are drawn; shots are fired. Billy's mother, an innocent bystander, is accidentally killed. Billy, a twelve-year-old, stabs the slayers without hesitation and flees, an outlaw.

Claude Debussy

Prelude to the Afternoon of a Faun

TERNARY FORM: ABA

Ex. 1 Principal theme.

Ex. 2 Theme of climax.

Ex. 3 Principal theme restated in augmentation.

Prelude to the Afternoon of a Faun. Permission for reprint granted by Editions Jean Jobert, Paris, France, copyright owners; Elkan-Vogel Co., Inc., Philadelphia, Pa., agent.

Franz Liszt

Les Préludes

The program that Liszt wrote for *Les Préludes* reads as follows:

"What is life but a series of preludes to that unknown song whose first solemn note is sounded by Death? Love is the enchanted dawn of every life, but what person is there whose first delights of happiness are not dissipated by some storm, a storm whose fatal blast dispels his youthful illusions, destroying his altar as though by a stroke of lightning? And what wounded soul, after the cruel storm, does not attempt to assuage its memories in the pleasant solitude of rural life? Nevertheless, man does not long allow himself the sweet quiet offered in Nature's bosom. When the trumpet sounds the alarm, he hurries to take up his post, no matter what struggle summons him, in order that in battle he may regain full confidence in himself and his powers."

Although *Les Préludes* is given a continuous performance, the work is divided into four contrasting sections.

Section I. Love, the Enchanted Dawn of Life

Ex. 1   Theme I. Basic motive in first three notes.

Variants of Theme I:

Ex. 2

Ex. 3

Ex. 4

219

Ex. 5

cresc.
strings

Ex. 6

ff brass, bassoons

Ex. 7

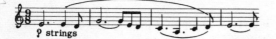

p strings

Ex. 8   Theme II.

p French horns

Ex. 9   Theme I recalled.

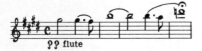

pp flute

Section II. Storms of Life

Ex. 10   Variant of Theme I, basic motive.

Allegro ma non troppo

p celli

Passages featuring tremolo and chromaticism.
Theme I, basic motive, repeated.

Section III. Rural Life Scene

Ex. 11.   Theme III.

Theme II restated, with Theme III as countermelody.

Section IV. Strife and Victory

Ex. 12   Variant of Theme I.

Ex. 13   Theme II in diminution.

Variant of Theme I (Ex. 6), restated.

Felix Mendelssohn

Concerto in E Minor for Violin and Orchestra, Op. 64

First Movement: Sonata-allegro form.

EXPOSITION

Ex. 1   Theme I.

Theme I repeated by orchestra.

Ex. 2   Transition theme.

Transition theme repeated by violin.

Ex. 3   Theme II.

Theme II repeated by violin. Closing theme.
Theme I restated by violin.

Ex. 4   Motive from Theme I developed by orchestra, accompanied by violin.

DEVELOPMENT

Development of beginning of Theme I by violin.
Short development of transition theme.

222

Ex. 5   Motive from Theme I developed by orchestra, accompanied by violin.

Cadenza for violin closes development.

RECAPITULATION

Ex. 6   Arpeggios at end of violin cadenza; Theme I in orchestra.

Abbreviated transition.
Remainder of section resembles exposition.

CODA

Begins as opening of development.
Tempo quickens.

Ex. 7   Transition theme developed.

Second Movement: Ternary form. ABA

Ex. 8

Ex. 9

Ex. 10   B, second statement.

A repeated.
Short coda.

Third movement: Sonata-allegro form.

INTRODUCTION

Ex. 11

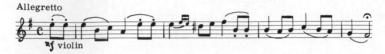

EXPOSITION

Ex. 12   Theme I.

Theme I repeated by violin.
Transition based on development of Theme I by orchestra, accompanied by rapid passages on violin.

Ex. 13   Theme II.

Theme II repeated by violin.

Ex. 14   Theme II in orchestra, accompanied by rapid passages on violin.

DEVELOPMENT

Theme I developed in new key by violin.

New countermelody for Theme I introduced by violin.

Ex. 15   Countermelody restated by orchestra while Theme I is developed by violin.

Staccato passage, by violin alone, closes development.

RECAPITULATION

Theme I restated by violin, with countermelody from development in orchestra.

Transition omitted.

Theme II, as in exposition.

CODA

Trills, violin alone.

Short reference to Theme I.

Theme II developed, concluding with a brilliant climax.

Modest Moussorgsky

Night on the Bare Mountain

Moussorgsky wrote the following program notes which are appended to the score:

"Subterranean sounds of supernatural voices."

Ex. 1

Ex. 2

"Appearance of the spirits of darkness, followed by that of the Black God."

Ex. 3

"Glorification of the Black God, the Black Mass. The Witches Sabbath . . ."

Ex. 4

Ex. 5

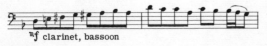

". . . interrupted at its height by the sounds of the bell of a distant village church. The spirits of darkness disperse."

Ex. 6

Poco meno mosso

"Daybreak."

Ex. 7

Meno mosso tranquillo

Giovanni Palestrina

Pope Marcellus Mass

Kyrie eleison

Ex. 1   This excerpt illustrates contrapuntal imitation of the subject, especially the imitation of the first few notes (see A).

Gloria

Ex. 2 The first line of the *Gloria* is chanted to a Gregorian melody by the celebrant of the Mass. Throughout the Gloria, the chordal style, in which the emphasis is on the harmonic element, predominates.

Sergei Rachmaninoff

Rhapsody on a Theme of Paganini, Op. 43

Theme and twenty-four variations. The theme is taken from the last of the Paganini *Caprices* for solo violin.

Ex. 1   Variation I. Outline of theme.

Ex. 2   Theme.

The following examples illustrate some of the techniques of variation used in this composition.

Ex. 3   Variation VII. Augmentation of theme in low strings; *Dies Irae*, chant from Requiem Mass (p. 155), by piano.

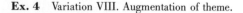

Ex. 4   Variation VIII. Augmentation of theme.

Rhapsody on a Theme of Paganini. Reprinted by permission of Charles Foley.

Ex. 5   Variation XII. Transformation of beginning of theme.

Ex. 6   Variation XIII. Augmentation, some rhythmic variation.

Ex. 7   Variation XVIII. Inversion of first five notes of theme as beginning of new melody.

Ex. 8   Coda. *Dies Irae* by orchestra; variation on theme by piano.

Maurice Ravel

"Daybreak" from *Daphnis and Chloe, Suite No. 2*

This part of the ballet is a pastoral scene at dawn. The sounds of a murmuring brook are heard as the scene opens:

Ex. 1

Little by little the dawn appears:

Ex. 2

The songs of birds are heard in the background. A shepherd enters announced by a short passage on the piccolo; another enters to a short tune on the clarinet. The dawn motive is heard growing into a new melody:

Ex. 3

As the day grows brighter, shepherds enter, finding Daphnis sleeping under the grotto of the nymphs. Daphnis, awakened, looks about anxiously for Chloe. She enters, surrounded by shepherdesses. Daphnis and Chloe embrace:

Ex. 4

Daphnis and Chloe. Permission for reprint granted by Durand et Cie, Paris, France, copyright owners; Elkan-Vogel Co., Inc., Philadelphia, Pa., agent.

Ottorino Respighi

Pines of Rome

Pines of Rome consists of four sections which are described as follows in the preface to the score.

The Pines of the Villa Borghese

"Children are playing in the pine groves of the Villa Borghese, dancing around and around; imitating soldiers, marching and fighting; their shrieking and shouting like the twittering of swallows at evening."

Ex. 1

Ex. 2

The Pines Near a Catacomb

"Without a pause between this and the preceding section, the scene shifts suddenly to the shadows of the pines overhanging the entrance to a catacomb. From the catacomb rises the sound of a solemn chant, which echoes again and again through the air, and then gradually and mysteriously disappears."

Ex. 3

Ex. 4

Pines of Rome. Copyright 1925 by G. Ricordi and Co. By permission.

Ex. 5

The Pines of the Janiculum

"A thrill of excitement runs through the air. The clear light of a full moon outlines the pines of the Janiculum. A nightingale is singing." (At this point a phonograph recording of a nightingale in song is used.)

Ex. 6

Ex. 7

The Pines of the Appian Way

"Misty dawn along the Appian Way. The magic countryside is guarded by solitary pines. There is heard the muffled rhythm of unending footsteps. The poet envisions in fantasy past glories; trumpets blast, and the returning victorious army advances in the brilliance of the newly-risen sun toward the Sacred Way, coming forth in triumph to the Capitol."

Ex. 8

Arnold Schoenberg

Quintet for Wind Instruments, Op. 26

Ex. 1 The tone row of the quintet.

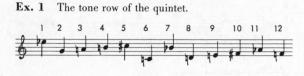

First Movement: Sonata-allegro form.

Ex. 2 First phrase. Principal theme uses first six tones of row; accompaniment uses last six tones.

Second Movement: Scherzo.

Ex. 3 Accompaniment uses first three tones of row; theme starts with fourth tone.

Third Movement: Ternary song form.

Ex. 4 Tone row appears in principal voice and contrapuntal voice.

Quintet for Wind Instruments, Op. 26. Copyright 1925 by Universal Edition, Vienna, renewed 1952 by Gertrud Schoenberg; used by permission of Associated Music Publishers, Inc., New York and Gertrud Schoenberg.

Fourth Movement: Rondo.

Ex. 5   Tone row is heard in principal voice; in accompaniment tone row is inverted at
octave.

Robert Schumann

Concerto in A Minor for Piano and Orchestra, Op. 54

First movement: Sonata-allegro form, with some characteristics of a fantasia.

EXPOSITION

Flourish of chords on piano.

Ex. 1   Theme I, motives A and B.

Theme I repeated by piano.
No transition.

Ex. 2   Theme II, motive C.

Theme II developed.

Ex. 3   Theme I in new key.

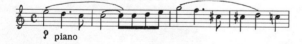

Ex. 4   Variant of Theme I.

Ex. 5   Development of motive C.

Ex. 6   Development of motive C.

f orchestra

DEVELOPMENT

Ex. 7   Theme I developed.

p piano, winds

Short reference to flourish of chords which opened movement.

Ex. 8   Theme I, motive A, developed.

p piano, flute

RECAPITULATION: closely resembles exposition.
    Cadenza at end of recapitulation.

Ex. 9   Beginning of cadenza. Motive B.

piano   *ff*   B

CODA

Ex. 10   Motive A in diminution.

p winds

Second Movement: Ternary form. ABA

Ex. 11   Based on motive B, first movement.

p piano

Ex. 12

𝅗𝅥𝅘𝅥 celli

A repeated.

Ex. 13   Transition to third movement. Motive A.

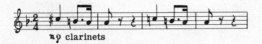

𝆏 clarinets

Third Movement: Sonata-allegro form.

EXPOSITION

Ex. 14   Theme I. Motive B from Theme I of first movement.

Allegro vivace   B

𝆑 piano   8𝆑

Transition.

Ex. 15   Theme II.

March-like

𝅗𝅥𝅘𝅥 strings

Ex. 16   Theme II repeated, legato phrasing.

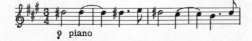

𝆏 piano

Theme II developed, conflicting rhythm in piano accompaniment.
Theme I restated by full orchestra.

DEVELOPMENT

Theme I developed by orchestra.

Ex. 17   New theme.

Theme I developed, alternating with development of new theme.

RECAPITULATION: closely resembles exposition.

CODA

Brilliant passages in piano.
Portion of Theme I developed.

Bedřich Smetana

The Moldau from *My Fatherland*

Smetana appended the following notes to the score:
"Two springs gush forth in the shade of the Bohemian forest, the one warm and spouting, the other cold and tranquil."

Ex. 1   Wave motive.

"Their ripples, gaily flowing over rocky beds, unite and glisten in the morning sun. The forest brook, rushing on, becomes the River Moldau, which, hurrying through Bohemia's valleys, grows into a mighty stream."

Ex. 2

"It flows through dense woods, where the joyous noise of the hunt and the tones of the hunter's horns sound nearer and nearer."

Ex. 3

"It flows through verdant meadows where a wedding feast is celebrated with song and dance."

Ex. 4

"At night the wood nymphs and water sprites revel in its glistening waves . . ."

Ex. 5

". . . which reflect many fortresses and castles—witnesses of the past splendor of chivalry and the vanished martial fame of bygone days."

Ex. 6

"At the rapids of St. John the stream speeds on, winding its way over cataracts and cutting a channel with its foaming waters through the rocky chasm . . ."

Ex. 7   Variation of the river melody.

". . . into the broad river bed in which it flows on in majestic calm . . ."

Ex. 8   River melody now in major key.

". . . toward Prague, welcomed by the time-honored Vysehrad" (famous Bohemian castle, citadel of the ancient kings).

Ex. 9   Vysehrad motive.

"It then disappears in the far distance from the poet's gaze."

Igor Stravinsky

Petrouchka

A carnival is the setting for the action in this ballet.

First Scene: The Carnival

Ex. 1   The carnival theme.

Ex. 2   A group of drunken revelers.

Ex. 3   Dancing girl entertaining the crowd.

Interest is drawn to a Magician and his three puppets: Petrouchka, the Ballerina, and the Moor. After a short solo on the flute with which the Magician lures the crowd to his booth, he animates the puppets and, to the delight of the astonished crowd, they perform a wild Russian dance:

Ex. 4

Second Scene: Petrouchka's Room

Petrouchka, the ugly clown, and the handsome Moor are both in love with the Ballerina. Petrouchka, his love unrequited, throws himself about his room in a fit of rage and frustration.

Petrouchka. Copyright by Edition Russe de Musique. Copyright assigned to Boosey and Hawkes Ltd. Revised version copyright 1947, 1948 by Boosey and Hawkes.

Ex. 5

Ex. 6

Third Scene: The Moor's Room

Ex. 7   Dance of the Moor.

Ex. 8   Entrance of the Ballerina.

Ex. 9   Waltz of the Ballerina and the Moor.

Petrouchka intrudes upon this romantic scene and is unceremoniously ejected by the infuriated Moor.

Fourth Scene: The Carnival

Various groups of dancers wend their way across the stage.

Ex. 10   Nurses' Dance.

The merrymaking comes to a halt when the Moor is seen chasing Petrouchka out of the Magician's booth. The Moor seizes Petrouchka and decapitates him with his sword. The crowd is horrified. The Magician appears to reassure the spectators that the puppets are only wood and sawdust. At the very end, however, Petrouchka's ghost, mocking and menacing, appears above the puppet booth for a brief moment. The crowd disperses.

Peter Ilich Tchaikovsky

Romeo and Juliet (Overture Fantasy)

Modified sonata-allegro form.

INTRODUCTION

Ex. 1 Friar Theme.

Friar Theme repeated, with pizzicato accompaniment on strings.
Non-thematic mood-setting phrases.
Accelerando.

EXPOSITION

Ex. 2 Strife Theme.

Strife Theme developed.
Rapid scale passages on strings.
Strife Theme repeated by full orchestra.
Long transition.

Ex. 3 Romeo Theme.

Ex. 4 Juliet Theme.

Romeo Theme repeated and extended.

DEVELOPMENT

Motive from Strife Theme developed.

Ex. 5   Rhythmic pattern from Strife Theme developed by strings; Friar Theme heard in horns.

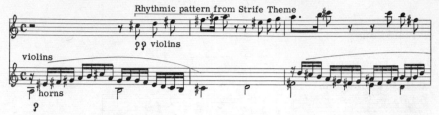

Ex. 6   Friar Theme in brass; rhythmic motive from Strife Theme in orchestra.

Development dissolves into recapitulation. Rapid scale passages on strings.

RECAPITULATION

Strife Theme restated by full orchestra.
Very short transition.
Juliet Theme heard in winds.
Rising scales on strings.
Romeo Theme restated by full orchestra.
Strife Theme interrupts Romeo Theme.
Strife and Friar Themes developed.

EPILOGUE

Reference to Romeo Theme by celli.

Ex. 7   Romeo Theme developed.

Index

Page numbers in boldface type indicate that a paragraph of text is devoted to each of the composers so listed.

247